MznLnx

Missing Links Exam Preps

Exam Prep for

Calculus with Applications: Brief Edition

Lial & Greenwell & Ritchey, 7th Edition

The MznLnx Exam Prep is your link from the texbook and lecture to your exams.
The MznLnx Exam Preps are unauthorized and comprehensive reviews of your textbooks.

All material provided by MznLnx and Rico Publications (c) 2010
Textbook publishers and textbook authors do not particpate in or contribute to these reviews.

MznLnx

Rico
Publications

Exam Prep for Calculus with Applications: Brief Edition
7th Edition
Lial & Greenwell & Ritchey

Publisher: Raymond Houge
Assistant Editor: Michael Rouger
Text and Cover Designer: Lisa Buckner
Marketing Manager: Sara Swagger
Project Manager, Editorial Production: Jerry Emerson
Art Director: Vernon Lowerui

Product Manager: Dave Mason
Editorial Assitant: Rachel Guzmanji
Pedagogy: Debra Long
Cover Image: Jim Reed/Getty Images
Text and Cover Printer: City Printing, Inc.
Compositor: Media Mix, Inc.

(c) 2010 Rico Publications
ALL RIGHTS RESERVED. No part of this work
covered by the copyright may be reproduced or
used in any form or by an means--graphic, electronic,
or mechanical, including photocopying, recording,
taping, Web distribution, information storage, and
retrieval systems, or in any other manner--without the
written permission of the publisher.

Printed in the United States
ISBN:

For more information about our products, contact us at:
Dave.Mason@RicoPublications.com

For permission to use material from this text or
product, submit a request online to:
Dave.Mason@RicoPublications.com

Contents

CHAPTER 1
LINEAR FUNCTIONS — 1

CHAPTER 2
NONLINEAR FUNCTIONS — 8

CHAPTER 3
THE DERIVATIVE — 18

CHAPTER 4
CALCULATING THE DERIVATIVE — 27

CHAPTER 5
GRAPHS AND THE DERIVATIVE — 35

CHAPTER 6
APPLICATIONS OF THE DERIVATIVE — 43

CHAPTER 7
INTEGRATION — 50

CHAPTER 8
FURTHER TECHNIQUES AND APPLICATIONS OF INTEGRATION — 60

CHAPTER 9
MULTIVARIABLE CALCULUS — 66

ANSWER KEY — 77

TO THE STUDENT

COMPREHENSIVE

The *MznLnx* Exam Prep series is designed to help you pass your exams. Editors at MznLnx review your textbooks and then prepare these practice exams to help you master the textbook material. Unlike study guides, workbooks, and practice tests provided by the texbook publisher and textbook authors, *MznLnx* gives you **all** of the material in each chapter in exam form, not just samples, so you can be sure to nail your exam.

MECHANICAL

The MznLnx Exam Prep series creates exams that will help you learn the subject matter as well as test you on your understanding. Each question is designed to help you master the concept. Just working through the exams, you gain an understanding of the subject--its a simple mechanical process that produces success.

INTEGRATED STUDY GUIDE AND REVIEW

MznLnx is not just a set of exams designed to test you, its also a comprehensive review of the subject content. Each exam question is also a review of the concept, making sure that you will get the answer correct without having to go to other sources of material. You learn as you go! Its the easiest way to pass an exam.

HUMOR

Studying can be tedious and dry. MznLnx's instructional design includes moderate humor within the exam questions on occassion, to break the tedium and revitalize the brain

Chapter 1. LINEAR FUNCTIONS

1. In mathematics, the _____ is used to determine each point uniquely in a plane through two numbers, usually called the x-coordinate or abscissa and the y-coordinate or ordinate of the point. To define the coordinates, two perpendicular directed lines, are specified, as well as the unit length, which is marked off on the two axes Cartesian coordinate systems are also used in space and in higher dimensions.
   a. Cylindrical coordinate system
   b. Coordinate
   c. 15 theorem
   d. Cartesian coordinate system

2. In mathematics and its applications, a _____ system is a system for assigning an n-tuple of numbers or scalars to each point in an n-dimensional space. This concept is part of the theory of manifolds. 'Scalars' in many cases means real numbers, but, depending on context, can mean complex numbers or elements of some other commutative ring.
   a. Spherical coordinate system
   b. Coordinate
   c. Cylindrical coordinate system
   d. 15 theorem

3. In computer science and information science, _____ could also be a method or an algorithm. Again, an example will illustrate: There are systems of counting, as with Roman numerals, and various systems for filing papers, or catalogues, and various library systems, of which the Dewey Decimal _____ is an example. This still fits with the definition of components which are connected together (in this case in order to facilitate the flow of information.)
   a. 15 theorem
   b. System
   c. BDDC
   d. BIBO stability

4. _____ is used to describe the steepness, incline, gradient, or grade of a straight line. A higher _____ value indicates a steeper incline. The _____ is defined as the ratio of the 'rise' divided by the 'run' between two points on a line, or in other words, the ratio of the altitude change to the horizontal distance between any two points on the line.
   a. Sequence
   b. Slope
   c. 15 theorem
   d. Y-intercept

Chapter 1. LINEAR FUNCTIONS

5. In mathematics, a (topological) _____ is defined as follows: let I be an interval of real numbers (i.e. a non-empty connected subset of $\mathbb{R}$); then a _____ γ is a continuous mapping $\gamma: I \to X$, where X is a topological space. The _____ γ is said to be simple if it is injective, i.e. if for all x, y in I, we have $\gamma(x) = \gamma(y) \implies x = y$. If I is a closed bounded interval $[a, b]$, we also allow the possibility $\gamma(a) = \gamma(b)$ (this convention makes it possible to talk about closed simple _____.)

a. Curve
b. Closed curve
c. Prolate cycloid
d. Tractrix

6. In coordinate geometry, the _____ is the y-value of the point where the graph of a function or relation intercepts the y-axis of the coordinate system.

In other words, the _____ of a function is the y-value of the point at which it intersects the line x=0 (the y-axis.) Thus, if the function is specified in form y = f(x), the _____ is easy to find by calculating f.

a. 15 theorem
b. Y-intercept
c. Sequence
d. Slope

7. A _____ is an algebraic equation in which each term is either a constant or the product of a constant and (the first power of) a single variable. Linear equations can have one, two, three or more variables. Linear equations occur with great regularity in applied mathematics.

a. Cubic function
b. Quadratic formula
c. Quartic function
d. Linear equation

8. A _____ is a type of display using Cartesian coordinates to display values for two variables for a set of data. The data is displayed as a collection of points, each having the value of one variable determining the position on the horizontal axis and the value of the other variable determining the position on the vertical axis.

a. 15 theorem
b. Scatter plot
c. BDDC
d. BIBO stability

Chapter 1. LINEAR FUNCTIONS

9. _____ is a type of motion in which the velocity of an object changes equal amounts in equal time periods. An example of an object having _____ would be a ball rolling down a ramp. The object picks up velocity as it goes down the ramp with equal changes in time.
   a. ALGOR
   b. AUSM
   c. ACTRAN
   d. Uniform Acceleration

10. The terms '_____' and 'independent variable' are used in similar but subtly different ways in mathematics and statistics as part of the standard terminology in those subjects. They are used to distinguish between two types of quantities being considered, separating them into those available at the start of a process and those being created by it, where the latter (dependent variables) are dependent on the former (independent variables.)

In traditional calculus, a function is defined as a relation between two terms called variables because their values vary.

   a. BDDC
   b. BIBO stability
   c. 15 theorem
   d. Dependent variable

11. The terms 'dependent variable' and '_____' are used in similar but subtly different ways in mathematics and statistics as part of the standard terminology in those subjects. They are used to distinguish between two types of quantities being considered, separating them into those available at the start of a process and those being created by it, where the latter (dependent variables) are dependent on the former (independent variables.)

In traditional calculus, a function is defined as a relation between two terms called variables because their values vary.

   a. ALGOR
   b. AUSM
   c. ACTRAN
   d. Independent variable

12. In physics, _____ is movement that changes the position of an object, as opposed to rotation. For example, according to Whittaker:

Chapter 1. LINEAR FUNCTIONS

A _____ is the operation changing the positions of all points (x, y, z) of an object according to the formula

$$(x, y, z) \rightarrow (x + \Delta x, y + \Delta y, z + \Delta z)$$

where $(\Delta x, \Delta y, \Delta z)$ is the same vector for each point of the object. The _____ vector $(\Delta x, \Delta y, \Delta z)$ common to all points of the object describes a particular type of displacement of the object, usually called a linear displacement to distinguish it from displacements involving rotation, called angular displacements.

a. 15 theorem
b. BIBO stability
c. Translation
d. BDDC

13. The method of _____ or ordinary _____ is used to solve overdetermined systems. _____ is often applied in statistical contexts, particularly regression analysis.

_____ can be interpreted as a method of fitting data. The best fit in the _____ sense is that instance of the model for which the sum of squared residuals has its least value, a residual being the difference between an observed value and the value given by the model.

a. Least squares
b. 15 theorem
c. BIBO stability
d. BDDC

14. In statistics, _____ is a form of regression analysis in which the relationship between one or more independent variables and another variable, called dependent variable, is modeled by a least squares function, called _____ equation. This function is a linear combination of one or more model parameters, called regression coefficients. A _____ equation with one independent variable represents a straight line.
a. Probability
b. Correlation
c. Standard deviation
d. Linear regression

Chapter 1. LINEAR FUNCTIONS

15. In economics, the _____ functional form of production functions is widely used to represent the relationship of an output to inputs. It was proposed by Knut Wicksell (1851-1926), and tested against statistical evidence by Charles Cobb and Paul Douglas in 1900-1928.

For production, the function is

$Y = AL^{\alpha}K^{\beta}$,

where:

- Y = total production (the monetary value of all goods produced in a year)
- L = labor input
- K = capital input
- A = total factor productivity
- α and β are the output elasticities of labor and capital, respectively. These values are constants determined by available technology.

Output elasticity measures the responsiveness of output to a change in levels of either labor or capital used in production, ceteris paribus. For example if $\alpha = 0.15$, a 1% increase in labor would lead to approximately a 0.15% increase in output.

a. 15 theorem
b. BDDC
c. BIBO stability
d. Cobb-Douglas

16. In mathematics, the simplest case of _____ refers to the study of problems in which one seeks to minimize or maximize a real function by systematically choosing the values of real or integer variables from within an allowed set. This (a scalar real valued objective function) is actually a small subset of this field which comprises a large area of applied mathematics and generalizes to study of means to obtain 'best available' values of some objective function given a defined domain where the elaboration is on the types of functions and the conditions and nature of the objects in the problem domain.

The first _____ technique, which is known as steepest descent, goes back to Gauss.

a. Optimization
b. ACTRAN
c. AUSM
d. ALGOR

Chapter 1. LINEAR FUNCTIONS

17. In mathematics, the _____ (or modulus) of a real number is its numerical value without regard to its sign. So, for example, 3 is the _____ of both 3 and −3.

The _____ of a number a is denoted by $|a|$.

a. ACTRAN
b. Exponential function
c. Area hyperbolic functions
d. Absolute value

18. In mathematics, a _____ is a polynomial equation of the second degree. The general form is

$$ax^2 + bx + c = 0,$$

where a ≠ 0.

Students and teachers all over the world are familiar with the quadratic formula that can be derived by completing the square.

a. Stern-Brocot tree
b. Lochs' theorem
c. Continued fraction
d. Quadratic equation

19. _____ is the addition of a set of numbers; the result is their sum or total. An interim or present total of a _____ process is termed the running total. The 'numbers' to be summed may be natural numbers, complex numbers, matrices, or still more complicated objects.

a. BIBO stability
b. 15 theorem
c. BDDC
d. Summation

20. In mathematics, a _____ is a constant multiplicative factor of a certain object. For example, in the expression $9x^2$, the _____ of x^2 is 9.

The object can be such things as a variable, a vector, a function, etc.

a. Degree of the polynomial
b. Resultant
c. Binomial type
d. Coefficient

21. In probability theory and statistics, _____ indicates the strength and direction of a linear relationship between two random variables. That is in contrast with the usage of the term in colloquial speech, denoting any relationship, not necessarily linear. In general statistical usage, _____ or co-relation refers to the departure of two random variables from independence.
    a. Continuous random variable
    b. Standard deviation
    c. Geometric mean
    d. Correlation

22. A _____ is a statement of the meaning of a word or phrase. The term to be defined is known as the definiendum . The words which define it are known as the definiens .
    a. BDDC
    b. 15 theorem
    c. BIBO stability
    d. Definition

Chapter 2. NONLINEAR FUNCTIONS

1. In mathematics, the _____ (or replacement set) of a given function is the set of 'input' values for which the function is defined. For instance, the _____ of cosine would be all real numbers, while the _____ of the square root would be only numbers greater than or equal to 0 (ignoring complex numbers in both cases.) In a representation of a function in a xy Cartesian coordinate system, the _____ is represented on the x axis (or abscissa.)
   a. 15 theorem
   b. BDDC
   c. Domain
   d. BIBO stability

2. _____ is any physical or virtual entity that is owned by an individual or jointly by a group of individuals. An owner of _____ has the right to consume, sell, rent, mortgage, transfer and exchange his or her _____. Important widely-recognized types of _____ include real _____, personal _____ (other physical possessions), and intellectual _____ (rights over artistic creations, inventions, etc.), although the latter is not always as widely recognized or enforced.
   a. BIBO stability
   b. Property
   c. 15 theorem
   d. BDDC

3. In physics, _____ is movement that changes the position of an object, as opposed to rotation. For example, according to Whittaker:

   A _____ is the operation changing the positions of all points (x, y, z) of an object according to the formula

   $$(x, y, z) \rightarrow (x + \Delta x, y + \Delta y, z + \Delta z)$$

   where $(\Delta x, \Delta y, \Delta z)$ is the same vector for each point of the object. The _____ vector $(\Delta x, \Delta y, \Delta z)$ common to all points of the object describes a particular type of displacement of the object, usually called a linear displacement to distinguish it from displacements involving rotation, called angular displacements.

   a. BDDC
   b. 15 theorem
   c. BIBO stability
   d. Translation

4. The _____ is a test to determine if a relation or its graph is a function or not. For a relation or graph to be a function, it can have at most a single y-value for each x-value. Thus, a vertical line drawn at any x-position on the graph of a function will intersect the graph at most once.

Chapter 2. NONLINEAR FUNCTIONS

a. BIBO stability
b. Vertical line test
c. BDDC
d. 15 theorem

5. In mathematics, a function on the real numbers is called a _____ (or staircase function) if it can be written as a finite linear combination of indicator functions of intervals. Informally speaking, a _____ is a piecewise constant function having only finitely many pieces.

a. Multiplicative inverse
b. Hyperbolic sine
c. Square root function
d. Step function

6. In mathematics, the _____ is a conic section, the intersection of a right circular conical surface and a plane parallel to a generating straight line of that surface. Given a point (the focus) and a line (the directrix) that lie in a plane, the locus of points in that plane that are equidistant to them is a _____.

A particular case arises when the plane is tangent to the conical surface of a circle.

a. BIBO stability
b. 15 theorem
c. Parabola
d. BDDC

7. In mathematics, a _____ is a polynomial equation of the second degree. The general form is

$$ax^2 + bx + c = 0,$$

where a ≠ 0.

Students and teachers all over the world are familiar with the quadratic formula that can be derived by completing the square.

a. Lochs' theorem
b. Stern-Brocot tree
c. Continued fraction
d. Quadratic equation

8. A quadratic equation with real or complex coefficients has two solutions (or roots), not necessarily distinct, which may or may not be real, given by the _____:

$$\frac{-b \pm \sqrt{b^2 - 4ac}}{2a}$$

Example discriminant signsâ– <0: $x^2+\frac{1}{2}$â– =0: $-\frac{4}{3}x^2+\frac{4}{3}x-\frac{1}{3}$â– >0: $\frac{3}{2}x^2+\frac{1}{2}x-\frac{4}{3}$

In the above formula, the expression underneath the square root sign

$$D = b^2 - 4ac,$$

is called the discriminant of the quadratic equation.

A quadratic equation with real coefficients can have either one or two distinct real roots, or two distinct complex roots. In this case the discriminant determines the number and nature of the roots.

a. Cubic function
b. Linear equation
c. Quartic function
d. Quadratic formula

9. A _____, in mathematics, is a polynomial function of the form $f(x) = ax^2 + bx + c$, where $a \neq 0$. The graph of a _____ is a parabola whose major axis is parallel to the y-axis.

The expression ax² + bx + c in the definition of a _____ is a polynomial of degree 2 or a 2nd degree polynomial, because the highest exponent of x is 2.

a. Quadratic function
b. Resultant
c. Discriminant
d. Leading coefficient

10. _____ generally conveys two primary meanings. The first is an imprecise sense of harmonious or aesthetically-pleasing proportionality and balance; such that it reflects beauty or perfection. The second meaning is a precise and well-defined concept of balance or 'patterned self-similarity' that can be demonstrated or proved according to the rules of a formal system: by geometry, through physics or otherwise.

a. BIBO stability
b. BDDC
c. 15 theorem
d. Symmetry

11. In elementary algebra, _____ is a technique for converting a quadratic polynomial of the form

$$ax^2 + bx + c$$

to the form

$$a(\cdots\cdots)^2 + \text{constant}.$$

The expression inside the parenthesis is of the form x − constant. Thus one converts ax² + bx + c to

$$a(x - h)^2 + k$$

and one must find h and k.

_____ is used in

- solving quadratic equations,
- graphing quadratic functions,
- evaluating integrals in calculus,
- finding Laplace transforms.

In mathematics, _____ is considered a basic algebraic operation, and is often applied without remark in any computation involving quadratic polynomials.

There is a simple formula in elementary algebra for computing the square of a binomial:

$$(x + p)^2 = x^2 + 2px + p^2.$$

For example:

$$(x + 3)^2 = x^2 + 6x + 9 \qquad (p = 3)$$
$$(x - 5)^2 = x^2 - 10x + 25 \qquad (p = -5).$$

In any perfect square, the number p is always half the coefficient of x, and then the constant term is equal to p².

Chapter 2. NONLINEAR FUNCTIONS

    a. Multinomial theorem
    b. Completing the square
    c. Closed-form expression
    d. Hurwitz quaternion order

12. The principal _____ $f(x) = \sqrt{x}$ (usually just referred to as the '_____') is a function which maps the set of non-negative real numbers $R^+ \cup \{0\}$ onto itself, and, like all functions, always returns a unique value. The _____ also maps rational numbers into algebraic numbers (a superset of the rational numbers); $\sqrt{x}$ is rational if and only if x is a rational number which can be represented as a ratio of two perfect squares. In geometrical terms, the _____ maps the area of a square to its side length.
    a. Square root function
    b. Hyperbolic cosine
    c. Hyperbolic tangent
    d. Multiplicative inverse

13. In mathematics, a _____ is a constant multiplicative factor of a certain object. For example, in the expression $9x^2$, the _____ of x^2 is 9.

The object can be such things as a variable, a vector, a function, etc.

    a. Resultant
    b. Binomial type
    c. Degree of the polynomial
    d. Coefficient

14. When a polynomial is expressed as a sum or difference of terms (e.g., in standard or canonical form), the exponent of the term with the highest exponent is the _____. The degree of a term is the sum of the powers of each variable in the term. The words degree and order are used interchangeably.
    a. Symmetric function
    b. Quadratic polynomial
    c. Binomial type
    d. Degree of the polynomial

15. For the largest k where $a_k \neq 0$, a_k is called the _____ of P because most often, polynomials are written starting from the left with the largest power of x. So for example the _____ of the polynomial

Chapter 2. NONLINEAR FUNCTIONS

$$4x^5 + x^3 + 2x^2$$

is 4.

The coefficients of polynomial also may be in the other order:

$$Q(x) = a_0 x^k + a_1 x^{k-1} + \cdots + a_{k-1} x^1 + a_k$$

and must be $a_0 \neq 0$ and a_0 is the _____ of Q.

a. Symmetric function
b. Resultant
c. Discriminant
d. Leading coefficient

16. An _____ of a real-valued function y = f(x) is a curve which describes the behavior of f as either x or y tends to infinity.

In other words, as one moves along the graph of f(x) in some direction, the distance between it and the _____ eventually becomes smaller than any distance that one may specify.

a. ACTRAN
b. ALGOR
c. AUSM
d. Asymptote

17. In mathematics, _____ and minima, known collectively as extrema, are the largest value (maximum) or smallest value (minimum), that a function takes in a point either within a given neighbourhood (local extremum) or on the function domain in its entirety (global extremum.)

Throughout, a point refers to an input (x), while a value refers to an output (y): one distinguishing between the maximum value and the point (or points) at which it occurs.

A real-valued function f defined on the real line is said to have a local maximum point at the point x^*, if there exists some $\varepsilon > 0$, such that $f(x^*) \geq f(x)$ when $|x - x^*| < \varepsilon$.

a. Related rates
b. Leibniz formula
c. Racetrack principle
d. Maxima

18. In mathematics, a (topological) _____ is defined as follows: let I be an interval of real numbers (i.e. a non-empty connected subset of $\mathbb{R}$); then a _____ γ is a continuous mapping $\gamma : I \to X$, where X is a topological space. The _____ γ is said to be simple if it is injective, i.e. if for all x, y in I, we have $\gamma(x) = \gamma(y) \implies x = y$. If I is a closed bounded interval $[a, b]$, we also allow the possibility $\gamma(a) = \gamma(b)$ (this convention makes it possible to talk about closed simple _____.)
    a. Prolate cycloid
    b. Closed curve
    c. Tractrix
    d. Curve

19. _____ is the long dimension of any object. The _____ of a thing is the distance between its ends, its linear extent as measured from end to end. This may be distinguished from height, which is vertical extent, and width or breadth, which are the distance from side to side, measuring across the object at right angles to the _____.
    a. BDDC
    b. BIBO stability
    c. Length
    d. 15 theorem

20. A _____ is a statement of the meaning of a word or phrase. The term to be defined is known as the definiendum. The words which define it are known as the definiens.
    a. BIBO stability
    b. 15 theorem
    c. BDDC
    d. Definition

21. The _____ is a function in mathematics. The application of this function to a value x is written as exp(x). Equivalently, this can be written in the form e^x, where e is a mathematical constant, the base of the natural logarithm, which equals approximately 2.718281828, and is also known as Euler's number.

Chapter 2. NONLINEAR FUNCTIONS

a. Integral part
b. Exponential function
c. ACTRAN
d. Area hyperbolic functions

22. In mathematics, the _____ of a function y = f(x) is a function that, in some fashion, 'undoes' the effect of f The _____ of f is denoted f⁻¹. The statements y=f(x) and x=f⁻¹(y) are equivalent.
    a. AUSM
    b. Inverse
    c. ALGOR
    d. ACTRAN

23. In mathematics, if f is a function from A to B then an _____ for f is a function in the opposite direction, from B to A, with the property that a round trip (a composition) from A to B to A (or from B to A to B) returns each element of the initial set to itself. Thus, if an input x into the function f produces an output y, then inputting y into the _____ f^{-1} (read f inverse, not to be confused with exponentiation) produces the output x. Not every function has an inverse; those that do are called invertible.
    a. Aristotle
    b. Augustin-Jean Fresnel
    c. Inverse function
    d. Augustin Louis Cauchy

24. The _____, formerly known as the hyperbolic logarithm, is the logarithm to the base e, where e is an irrational constant approximately equal to 2.718281828. It is also sometimes referred to as the Napierian logarithm, although the original meaning of this term is slightly different. In simple terms, the _____ of a number x is the power to which e would have to be raised to equal x -- for example the natural log of e itself is 1 because e^1 = e, while the _____ of 1 would be 0, since e^0 = 1.
    a. BDDC
    b. 15 theorem
    c. BIBO stability
    d. Natural logarithm

25. _____ is a type of motion in which the velocity of an object changes equal amounts in equal time periods. An example of an object having _____ would be a ball rolling down a ramp. The object picks up velocity as it goes down the ramp with equal changes in time.

Chapter 2. NONLINEAR FUNCTIONS

a. ACTRAN
b. Uniform Acceleration
c. AUSM
d. ALGOR

26. The _____ of a quantity whose value decreases with time is the interval required for the quantity to decay to half of its initial value. The concept originated in describing how long it takes atoms to undergo radioactive decay but also applies in a wide variety of other situations.

The term '_____' dates to 1907.

a. Half-life
b. 15 theorem
c. BDDC
d. BIBO stability

27. _____ (including exponential decay) occurs when the growth rate of a mathematical function is proportional to the function's current value. In the case of a discrete domain of definition with equal intervals it is also called geometric growth or geometric decay (the function values form a geometric progression.)

_____ is said to follow an exponential law; the simple-_____ model is known as the Malthusian growth model.

a. Isomonodromic deformation
b. Inseparable differential equation
c. Exponential growth
d. Oscillating

28. In mathematics, a _____ is a function which preserves the given order. This concept first arose in calculus, and was later generalized to the more abstract setting of order theory.

In calculus, a function f defined on a subset of the real numbers with real values is called monotonic (also monotonically increasing or non-decreasing), if for all x and y such that x >≤ y one has f(x) >≤ f(y), so f preserves the order.

a. Pseudo-differential operator
b. Pettis integral
c. 15 theorem
d. Monotonic function

29. In calculus, a branch of mathematics, the _____ is a measurement of how a function changes when its input changes. Loosely speaking, a _____ can be thought of as how much a quantity is changing at some given point. For example, the _____ of the position (or distance) of a vehicle with respect to time is the instantaneous velocity (respectively, instantaneous speed) at which the vehicle is traveling.

The process of finding a _____ is called differentiation. The fundamental theorem of calculus states that differentiation is the reverse process to integration.

a. Bounded function
b. Derivative
c. Stationary phase approximation
d. Semi-differentiability

Chapter 3. THE DERIVATIVE

1. In mathematics, the concept of a '_____' is used to describe the behavior of a function as its argument or input either 'gets close' to some point, or as the argument becomes arbitrarily large; or the behavior of a sequence's elements as their index increases indefinitely. Limits are used in calculus and other branches of mathematical analysis to define derivatives and continuity.

   In formulas, _____ is usually abbreviated as lim

   a. BDDC
   b. 15 theorem
   c. BIBO stability
   d. Limit

2. In mathematics, the _____ is a fundamental concept in calculus and analysis concerning the behavior of that function near a particular input. Informally, a function assigns an output f(x) to every input x. The function has a limit L at an input p if f(x) is 'close' to L whenever x is 'close' to p.
   a. 15 theorem
   b. Table of limits
   c. Squeeze Theorem
   d. Limit of a function

3. In calculus, a _____ is either of the two limits of a function f(x) of a real variable x as x approaches a specified point either from below or from above. One should write either:

   $$\lim_{x \to a^+} f(x) \text{ or } \lim_{x \downarrow a} f(x)$$

   for the limit as x decreases in value approaching a (x approaches a 'from above' or 'from the right'), and similarly

   $$\lim_{x \to a^-} f(x) \text{ or } \lim_{x \uparrow a} f(x)$$

   for the limit as x increases in value approaching a (x approaches a 'from below' or 'from the left'.)

   The two one-sided limits exist and are equal if and only if the limit of f(x) as x approaches a exists.

   a. ACTRAN
   b. ALGOR
   c. AUSM
   d. One-sided limit

Chapter 3. THE DERIVATIVE 19

4. In physics, _____ is movement that changes the position of an object, as opposed to rotation. For example, according to Whittaker:

A _____ is the operation changing the positions of all points (x, y, z) of an object according to the formula

$$(x, y, z) \to (x + \Delta x, y + \Delta y, z + \Delta z)$$

where $(\Delta x, \Delta y, \Delta z)$ is the same vector for each point of the object. The _____ vector $(\Delta x, \Delta y, \Delta z)$ common to all points of the object describes a particular type of displacement of the object, usually called a linear displacement to distinguish it from displacements involving rotation, called angular displacements.

a. 15 theorem
b. BIBO stability
c. BDDC
d. Translation

5. In calculus, a branch of mathematics, the _____ is a measurement of how a function changes when its input changes. Loosely speaking, a _____ can be thought of as how much a quantity is changing at some given point. For example, the _____ of the position (or distance) of a vehicle with respect to time is the instantaneous velocity (respectively, instantaneous speed) at which the vehicle is traveling.

The process of finding a _____ is called differentiation. The fundamental theorem of calculus states that differentiation is the reverse process to integration.

a. Bounded function
b. Stationary phase approximation
c. Semi-differentiability
d. Derivative

6. In economics, the _____ functional form of production functions is widely used to represent the relationship of an output to inputs. It was proposed by Knut Wicksell (1851-1926), and tested against statistical evidence by Charles Cobb and Paul Douglas in 1900-1928.

For production, the function is

$$Y = AL^{\alpha}K^{\beta},$$

where:

- Y = total production (the monetary value of all goods produced in a year)
- L = labor input
- K = capital input
- A = total factor productivity
- α and β are the output elasticities of labor and capital, respectively. These values are constants determined by available technology.

Output elasticity measures the responsiveness of output to a change in levels of either labor or capital used in production, ceteris paribus. For example if α = 0.15, a 1% increase in labor would lead to approximately a 0.15% increase in output.

   a. Cobb-Douglas
   b. 15 theorem
   c. BIBO stability
   d. BDDC

7. In mathematics, a _____ is a function for which, intuitively, small changes in the input result in small changes in the output. Otherwise, a function is said to be discontinuous. A _____ with a continuous inverse function is called bicontinuous. An intuitive though imprecise (and inexact) idea of continuity is given by the common statement that a _____ is a function whose graph can be drawn without lifting the chalk from the blackboard.
   a. Binomial series
   b. Hyperbolic angle
   c. Visual Calculus
   d. Continuous function

8. Continuous functions are of utmost importance in mathematics and applications. However, not all functions are continuous. If a function is not continuous at a point in its domain, one says that it has a _____ there. The set of all points of _____ of a function may be a discrete set, a dense set, or even the entire domain of the function.
   a. BDDC
   b. Vector
   c. 15 theorem
   d. Discontinuity

9. In metric topology and related fields of mathematics, a set U is called _____ if, intuitively speaking, starting from any point x in U one can move by a small amount in any direction and still be in the set U. In other words, the distance between any point x in U and the edge of U is always greater than zero.

Chapter 3. THE DERIVATIVE   21

As an example, consider the _____ interval (0, 1) consisting of all real numbers x with 0 < x < 1. Here, the topology is the usual topology on the real line. We can look at this in two ways.

   a. ACTRAN
   b. ALGOR
   c. AUSM
   d. Open

10.   An _____ of a real-valued function y = f(x) is a curve which describes the behavior of f as either x or y tends to infinity.

In other words, as one moves along the graph of f(x) in some direction, the distance between it and the _____ eventually becomes smaller than any distance that one may specify.

   a. AUSM
   b. ACTRAN
   c. Asymptote
   d. ALGOR

11.   In mathematics, a _____ is a function whose definition is dependent on the value of the independent variable. Mathematically, a real-valued function f of a real variable x is a relationship whose definition is given differently on disjoint subsets of its domain

The word piecewise is also used to describe any property of a _____ that holds for each piece but may not hold for the whole domain of the function.

   a. Range
   b. Constant function
   c. Piecewise-defined function
   d. Surjective

Chapter 3. THE DERIVATIVE

12. In mathematical analysis, the _____ states that for each value between the least upper bound and greatest lower bound of the image of a continuous function there is a corresponding value in its domain mapping to the original. _____

   - Version I. The _____ states the following: If the function y = f(x) is continuous on the interval [a, b], and u is a number between f(a) and f(b), then there is a c ∈ [a, b] such that f(c) = u.

   - Version II. Suppose that I is an interval [a, b] in the real numbers R and that f : I → R is a continuous function. Then the image set f(I) is also an interval, and either it contains [f(a), f(b)], or it contains [f(b), f(a)]; that is,

      f(I) ⊇ [f(a), f(b)], or f(I) ⊇ [f(b), f(a)].

   It is frequently stated in the following equivalent form: Suppose that f : [a, b] → R is continuous and that u is a real number satisfying f(a) < u < f(b) or f(a) > u > f(b.) Then for some c ∈ [a, b], f(c) = u.

   This captures an intuitive property of continuous functions: given f continuous on [1, 2], if f(1) = 3 and f(2) = 5 then f must take the value 4 somewhere between 1 and 2.

   a. ALGOR
   b. ACTRAN
   c. AUSM
   d. Intermediate value theorem

13. The function difference divided by the point difference is known as the _____, it is also known as Newton's quotient):

$$\frac{\Delta F(P)}{\Delta P} = \frac{F(P + \Delta P) - F(P)}{\Delta P} = \frac{\nabla F(P + \Delta P)}{\Delta P}.$$

If ΔP is infinitesimal, then the _____ is a derivative, otherwise it is a divided difference:

$$\text{If } |\Delta P| = iota: \quad \frac{\Delta F(P)}{\Delta P} = \frac{dF(P)}{dP} = F'(P) = G(P);$$

$$\text{If } |\Delta P| > iota: \quad \frac{\Delta F(P)}{\Delta P} = \frac{DF(P)}{DP} = F[P, P + \Delta P].$$

Chapter 3. THE DERIVATIVE

Regardless if ΔP is infinitesimal or finite, there is (at least--in the case of the derivative--theoretically) a point range, where the boundaries are $P \pm (.5)\Delta P$ (depending on the orientation--$\Delta F(P)$, $\delta F(P)$ or $\nabla F(P)$):

LB = Lower Boundary; UB = Upper Boundary;

Anyone familiar with derivatives knows that they can be regarded as functions themselves, harboring their own derivatives. Thus each function is home to sequential degrees ('higher orders') of derivation, or differentiation. This property can be generalized to all difference quotients. As this sequencing requires a corresponding boundary splintering, it is practical to break up the point range into smaller, equi-sized sections, with each section being marked by an intermediary point ('P_i'), where LB = P_0 and UB = P_{A_n}, the nth point, equaling the degree/order:

$LB = P_0 = P_0 + 0\Delta_1 P = P_{A_n} - (Åf-0)\Delta_1 P$; $P_1 = P_0 + 1\Delta_1 P = P_{A_n} - (Åf-1)\Delta_1 P$; $P_2 = P_0 + 2\Delta_1 P = P_{A_n} - (Åf-2)\Delta_1 P$; $P_3 = P_0 + 3\Delta_1 P = P_{A_n} - (Åf-3)\Delta_1 P$; ↓↓↓↓ $P_{A_n-3} = P_0 + (Åf-3)\Delta_1 P = P_{A_n} - 3\Delta_1 P$; $P_{A_n-2} = P_0 + (Åf-2)\Delta_1 P = P_{A_n} - 2\Delta_1 P$; $P_{A_n-1} = P_0 + (Åf-1)\Delta_1 P = P_{A_n} - 1\Delta_1 P$; $UB = P_{A_n-0} = P_0 + (Åf-0)\Delta_1 P = P_{A_n} - 0\Delta_1 P = P_{A_n}$;

$\Delta P = \Delta_1 P = P_1 - P_0 = P_2 - P_1 = P_3 - P_2 = ...$

  a. Continuously differentiable
  b. Directional derivative
  c. Notation for differentiation
  d. Difference quotient

14. In physics, _____ is defined as the rate of change of position. it is vector physical quantity; both speed and direction are required to define it. In the SI (metric) system, it is measured in meters per second: (m/s) or ms^{-1}.
  a. BDDC
  b. 15 theorem
  c. BIBO stability
  d. Velocity

15. A _____ of a curve is a line that (locally) intersects two points on the curve. The word secant comes from the Latin secare, for to cut.

It can be used to approximate the tangent to a curve, at some point P. If the secant to a curve is defined by two points, P and Q, with P fixed and Q variable, as Q approaches P along the curve, the direction of the secant approaches that of the tangent at P, assuming there is just one.

a. Secant line
b. Kappa curve
c. Witch of Agnesi
d. Curve

16. In geometry, the _____ (or simply the tangent) to a curve at a given point is the straight line that 'just touches' the curve at that point (in the sense explained more precisely below.) As it passes through the point of tangency, the _____ is 'going in the same direction' as the curve, and in this sense it is the best straight-line approximation to the curve at that point. The same definition applies to space curves and curves in n-dimensional Euclidean space.
    a. North pole
    b. Lie derivative
    c. Minimal surface
    d. Tangent line

17. In mathematics, a (topological) _____ is defined as follows: let I be an interval of real numbers (i.e. a non-empty connected subset of $\mathbb{R}$); then a _____ γ is a continuous mapping $\gamma : I \to X$, where X is a topological space. The _____ γ is said to be simple if it is injective, i.e. if for all x, y in I, we have $\gamma(x) = \gamma(y) \implies x = y$. If I is a closed bounded interval $[a, b]$, we also allow the possibility $\gamma(a) = \gamma(b)$ (this convention makes it possible to talk about closed simple _____.)
    a. Closed curve
    b. Prolate cycloid
    c. Tractrix
    d. Curve

18. A _____ is a statement of the meaning of a word or phrase. The term to be defined is known as the definiendum. The words which define it are known as the definiens.
    a. 15 theorem
    b. BDDC
    c. Definition
    d. BIBO stability

19. _____ is used to describe the steepness, incline, gradient, or grade of a straight line. A higher _____ value indicates a steeper incline. The _____ is defined as the ratio of the 'rise' divided by the 'run' between two points on a line, or in other words, the ratio of the altitude change to the horizontal distance between any two points on the line.

a. Y-intercept
b. Slope
c. 15 theorem
d. Sequence

20. In calculus, _____, was originally the use of expressions such as dx and dy and to represent 'infinitely small' (or infinitesimal) increments of quantities x and y, just as >Δx and >Δy represent finite increments of x and y respectively. So for y being a function of x, or

the derivative of y with respect to x, which later came to be viewed as

was, according to Leibniz, the quotient of an infinitesimal increment of y by an infinitesimal increment of x, or

where the right hand side is Lagrange's notation for the derivative of f at x.

Similarly, although mathematicians usually now view an integral

as a limit

where >Δx is an interval containing x_i, Leibniz viewed it as the sum (the integral sign denoting summation) of infinitely many infinitesimal quantities f(x) dx.

a. Smooth function
b. Time derivative
c. Stationary point
d. Leibniz's notation

21. In mathematics, the _____ (or modulus) of a real number is its numerical value without regard to its sign. So, for example, 3 is the _____ of both 3 and −3.

The _____ of a number a is denoted by $|a|$.

   a. Exponential function
   b. ACTRAN
   c. Area hyperbolic functions
   d. Absolute value

Chapter 4. CALCULATING THE DERIVATIVE

1. _____ is a type of motion in which the velocity of an object changes equal amounts in equal time periods. An example of an object having _____ would be a ball rolling down a ramp. The object picks up velocity as it goes down the ramp with equal changes in time.
   a. ALGOR
   b. ACTRAN
   c. AUSM
   d. Uniform Acceleration

2. In calculus, a branch of mathematics, the _____ is a measurement of how a function changes when its input changes. Loosely speaking, a _____ can be thought of as how much a quantity is changing at some given point. For example, the _____ of the position (or distance) of a vehicle with respect to time is the instantaneous velocity (respectively, instantaneous speed) at which the vehicle is traveling.

   The process of finding a _____ is called differentiation. The fundamental theorem of calculus states that differentiation is the reverse process to integration.

   a. Semi-differentiability
   b. Stationary phase approximation
   c. Bounded function
   d. Derivative

3. In elementary algebra, a _____ is a polynomial with two terms--the sum of two monomials--often bound by parenthesis or brackets when operated upon. It is the simplest kind of polynomial other than monomials.

   - The _____ $a^2 - b^2$ can be factored as the product of two other binomials:

     $a^2 - b^2 = (a + b)(a - b.)$

     This is a special case of the more general formula:

     $$a^{n+1} - b^{n+1} = (a - b) \sum_{k=0}^{n} a^k b^{n-k}$$

   - The product of a pair of linear binomials $(ax + b)$ and $(cx + d)$ is:

     $(ax + b)(cx + d) = acx^2 + axd + bcx + bd.$

   - A _____ raised to the nth power, represented as

     $(a + b)^n$

     can be expanded by means of the _____ theorem or, equivalently, using Pascal's triangle. Taking a simple example, the perfect square _____ $(p + q)^2$ can be found by squaring the :first digit, adding twice the product of the first and second digit and finally adding the square of the second digit, to give $p^2 + 2pq + q^2$.

a. Multinomial theorem
b. Completing the square
c. Partial fractions
d. Binomial

4. In mathematics, the _____ is an important formula giving the expansion of powers of sums. Its simplest version states that

$$(x+y)^n = \sum_{k=0}^{n} \binom{n}{k} x^{n-k} y^k \qquad (1)$$

for any real or complex numbers x and y, and any non-negative integer n. The binomial coefficient appearing in (1) may be defined in terms of the factorial function n!:

$$\binom{n}{k} = \frac{n!}{k!\,(n-k)!}.$$

For example, here are the cases where 2 ≤ n ≤ 5:

$$(x+y)^2 = x^2 + 2xy + y^2$$
$$(x+y)^3 = x^3 + 3x^2y + 3xy^2 + y^3$$
$$(x+y)^4 = x^4 + 4x^3y + 6x^2y^2 + 4xy^3 + y^4$$
$$(x+y)^5 = x^5 + 5x^4y + 10x^3y^2 + 10x^2y^3 + 5xy^4 + y^5.$$

Formula (1) is valid more generally for any elements x and y of a semiring as long as xy = yx.

a. Hypergeometric identities
b. Trinomial expansion
c. Central binomial coefficient
d. Binomial theorem

5. In calculus, _____, was originally the use of expressions such as dx and dy and to represent 'infinitely small' (or infinitesimal) increments of quantities x and y, just as >Δx and >Δy represent finite increments of x and y respectively. So for y being a function of x, or

$$\boxed{x}>$$

the derivative of y with respect to x, which later came to be viewed as

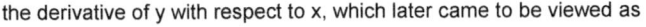

was, according to Leibniz, the quotient of an infinitesimal increment of y by an infinitesimal increment of x, or

where the right hand side is Lagrange's notation for the derivative of f at x.

Similarly, although mathematicians usually now view an integral

as a limit

where >Δx is an interval containing x_i, Leibniz viewed it as the sum (the integral sign denoting summation) of infinitely many infinitesimal quantities f(x) dx.

   a. Leibniz's notation
   b. Time derivative
   c. Stationary point
   d. Smooth function

6.   This article will state and prove the _____ for differentiation, and then use it to prove these two formulas.

The _____ for differentiation states that for every natural number n, the derivative of $f(x) = x^n$ is $f'(x) = nx^{n-1}$, that is,

$$(x^n)' = nx^{n-1}.$$

The _____ for integration

$$\int x^n \, dx = \frac{x^{n+1}}{n+1} + C$$

for natural n is then an easy consequence. One just needs to take the derivative of this equality and use the _____ and linearity of differentiation on the right-hand side.

a. Test for Divergence
b. Leibniz rule
c. Functional integration
d. Power rule

7. In calculus, the _____ is a formula used to find the derivatives of products of functions. It may be stated thus:

$$(f \cdot g)' = f' \cdot g + f \cdot g'$$

or in the Leibniz notation thus:

$$\frac{d}{dx}(u \cdot v) = u \cdot \frac{dv}{dx} + v \cdot \frac{du}{dx}.$$

Discovery of this rule is credited to Gottfried Leibniz, who demonstrated it using differentials. Here is Leibniz's argument: Let u and v be two differentiable functions of x.

a. Constant factor rule in differentiation
b. Differentiation rules
c. Product rule
d. Quotient Rule

8. In calculus, the _____ is a method of finding the derivative of a function that is the quotient of two other functions for which derivatives exist.

If the function one wishes to differentiate, f(x), can be written as

$$f(x) = \frac{g(x)}{h(x)}$$

Chapter 4. CALCULATING THE DERIVATIVE

and h(x) ≠ 0, then the rule states that the derivative of g(x) / h(x) is equal to:

$$\frac{d}{dx}f(x) = f'(x) = \frac{g'(x)h(x) - g(x)h'(x)}{[h(x)]^2}.$$

Or, more precisely, if all x in some open set containing the number a satisfy h(x) ≠ 0; and g'(a) and h'(a) both exist; then, f'(a) exists as well and:

$$f'(a) = \frac{g'(a)h(a) - g(a)h'(a)}{[h(a)]^2}.$$

The derivative of (4x − 2) / (x² + 1) is:

$$\frac{d}{dx}\left[\frac{(4x-2)}{x^2+1}\right] = \frac{(x^2+1)(4) - (4x-2)(2x)}{(x^2+1)^2}$$
$$= \frac{(4x^2+4) - (8x^2-4x)}{(x^2+1)^2} = \frac{-4x^2+4x+4}{(x^2+1)^2}$$

In the example above, the choices

g(x) = 4x − 2
h(x) = x² + 1

were made. Analogously, the derivative of sin(x) / x² (when x ≠ 0) is:

$$\frac{\cos(x)x^2 - \sin(x)2x}{x^4}$$

Another example is:

$$f(x) = \frac{2x^2}{x^3}$$

whereas g(x) = 2x² and h(x) = x³, and g'(x) = 4x and h'(x) = 3x².

a. Quotient rule
b. Constant factor rule in differentiation
c. Reciprocal Rule
d. Differentiation rules

9. In economics, _____ is equal to total cost divided by the number of goods produced (the output quantity, Q.) It is also equal to the sum of average variable costs (total variable costs divided by Q) plus average fixed costs (total fixed costs divided by Q.) Average costs may be dependent on the time period considered (increasing production may be expensive or impossible in the short term, for example.)
a. AUSM
b. ACTRAN
c. ALGOR
d. Average cost

10. In economics, the _____ functional form of production functions is widely used to represent the relationship of an output to inputs. It was proposed by Knut Wicksell (1851-1926), and tested against statistical evidence by Charles Cobb and Paul Douglas in 1900-1928.

For production, the function is

$$Y = AL^{\alpha}K^{\beta},$$

where:

- Y = total production (the monetary value of all goods produced in a year)
- L = labor input
- K = capital input
- A = total factor productivity
- α and β are the output elasticities of labor and capital, respectively. These values are constants determined by available technology.

Output elasticity measures the responsiveness of output to a change in levels of either labor or capital used in production, ceteris paribus. For example if α = 0.15, a 1% increase in labor would lead to approximately a 0.15% increase in output.

a. BDDC
b. 15 theorem
c. BIBO stability
d. Cobb-Douglas

Chapter 4. CALCULATING THE DERIVATIVE

11. In mathematics, a _____ represents the application of one function to the results of another. For instance, the functions f: X → Y and g: Y → Z can be composed by first computing f(x) and then applying a function g to the output of f(x.)

Thus one obtains a function g ∘ f: X → Z defined by (g ∘ f)(x) = g(f(x)) for all x in X. The notation g ∘ f is read as 'g circle f', or 'g composed with f', 'g after f', 'g following f', or just 'g of f'.

a. Piecewise-defined function
b. Constant function
c. Surjective
d. Composite function

12. In a totally ordered set all elements are mutually comparable, so such a set can have at most one minimal element and at most one maximal element. Then, due to mutual comparability, the minimal element will also be the least element and the maximal element will also be the greatest element. Thus in a totally ordered set we can simply use the terms minimum and _____.

a. Maximum
b. Leibniz rule
c. Racetrack principle
d. Nth term

13. In calculus, the _____ is a formula for the derivative of the composite of two functions.

In intuitive terms, if a variable, y, depends on a second variable, u, which in turn depends on a third variable, x, then the rate of change of y with respect to x can be computed as the rate of change of y with respect to u multiplied by the rate of change of u with respect to x. Schematically,

$$\frac{dy}{dx} = \frac{dy}{du} \cdot \frac{du}{dx}.$$

a. Differentiation rules
b. Chain rule
c. Product rule
d. Reciprocal Rule

14. A _____ officer is an officer of high military rank. The term or equivalent is used by nearly every country in the world. _____ can be used as a generic term for all grades of _____ officer, or it can specifically refer to a single rank that is just called _____.

a. BDDC
b. 15 theorem
c. BIBO stability
d. General

15. The _____ is a function in mathematics. The application of this function to a value x is written as exp(x). Equivalently, this can be written in the form e^x, where e is a mathematical constant, the base of the natural logarithm, which equals approximately 2.718281828, and is also known as Euler's number.
    a. Integral part
    b. Exponential function
    c. Area hyperbolic functions
    d. ACTRAN

16. A _____ or logistic curve is the most common sigmoid curve. It models the S-curve of growth of some set P, where P might be thought of as population. The initial stage of growth is approximately exponential; then, as saturation begins, the growth slows, and at maturity, growth stops.
    a. 15 theorem
    b. Logarithmic integral function
    c. Multiplication theorem
    d. Logistic function

17. The function $\log_b(x)$ depends on both b and x, but the term _____ in standard usage refers to a function of the form $\log_b(x)$ in which the base b is fixed and so the only argument is x. Thus there is one _____ for each value of the base b (which must be positive and must differ from 1.) Viewed in this way, the base-b _____ is the inverse function of the exponential function b^x.
    a. BIBO stability
    b. Logarithm function
    c. BDDC
    d. 15 theorem

Chapter 5. GRAPHS AND THE DERIVATIVE

1. In a totally ordered set all elements are mutually comparable, so such a set can have at most one minimal element and at most one maximal element. Then, due to mutual comparability, the minimal element will also be the least element and the maximal element will also be the greatest element. Thus in a totally ordered set we can simply use the terms _____ and maximum.
   a. Nth term
   b. Maximum
   c. Ghosts of departed quantities
   d. Minimum

2. _____ is used to describe the steepness, incline, gradient, or grade of a straight line. A higher _____ value indicates a steeper incline. The _____ is defined as the ratio of the 'rise' divided by the 'run' between two points on a line, or in other words, the ratio of the altitude change to the horizontal distance between any two points on the line.
   a. Sequence
   b. 15 theorem
   c. Y-intercept
   d. Slope

3. In geometry, the _____ (or simply the tangent) to a curve at a given point is the straight line that 'just touches' the curve at that point (in the sense explained more precisely below.) As it passes through the point of tangency, the _____ is 'going in the same direction' as the curve, and in this sense it is the best straight-line approximation to the curve at that point. The same definition applies to space curves and curves in n-dimensional Euclidean space.
   a. Minimal surface
   b. North pole
   c. Lie derivative
   d. Tangent line

4. In mathematics, a (topological) _____ is defined as follows: let I be an interval of real numbers (i.e. a non-empty connected subset of $\mathbb{R}$); then a _____ γ is a continuous mapping $\gamma : I \to X$, where X is a topological space. The _____ γ is said to be simple if it is injective, i.e. if for all x, y in I, we have $\gamma(x) = \gamma(y) \implies x = y$. If I is a closed bounded interval $[a, b]$, we also allow the possibility $\gamma(a) = \gamma(b)$ (this convention makes it possible to talk about closed simple _____.)
   a. Closed curve
   b. Tractrix
   c. Prolate cycloid
   d. Curve

5. In a totally ordered set all elements are mutually comparable, so such a set can have at most one minimal element and at most one maximal element. Then, due to mutual comparability, the minimal element will also be the least element and the maximal element will also be the greatest element. Thus in a totally ordered set we can simply use the terms minimum and _____.

a. Nth term
b. Racetrack principle
c. Leibniz rule
d. Maximum

6. In mathematics, a _____ is a function which preserves the given order. This concept first arose in calculus, and was later generalized to the more abstract setting of order theory.

In calculus, a function f defined on a subset of the real numbers with real values is called monotonic (also monotonically increasing or non-decreasing), if for all x and y such that x >≤ y one has f(x) >≤ f(y), so f preserves the order.

a. Pettis integral
b. 15 theorem
c. Pseudo-differential operator
d. Monotonic function

7. In physics, _____ is movement that changes the position of an object, as opposed to rotation. For example, according to Whittaker:

A _____ is the operation changing the positions of all points (x, y, z) of an object according to the formula

$$(x, y, z) \to (x + \Delta x, y + \Delta y, z + \Delta z)$$

where $(\Delta x, \Delta y, \Delta z)$ is the same vector for each point of the object. The _____ vector $(\Delta x, \Delta y, \Delta z)$ common to all points of the object describes a particular type of displacement of the object, usually called a linear displacement to distinguish it from displacements involving rotation, called angular displacements.

a. BIBO stability
b. 15 theorem
c. BDDC
d. Translation

Chapter 5. GRAPHS AND THE DERIVATIVE   37

8. In mathematics, a _____ (or critical number) is a point on the domain of a function where:

   - one dimension: the derivative (or slope of the line when visualized) is equal to zero or a point where the function ceases to be differentiable.
   - in general: there are two distinct concepts: either the derivative (Jacobian) vanishes, or it is not of full rank (or, in either case, the function is not differentiable); these agree in one dimension.

Note that in one dimension, a critical value or critical number x of function f is the domain element at which the derivative is zero or undefined, whereas the associated ordered pair (x, y) is the _____. In higher dimensions a critical value is in the range whereas a _____ is in the domain.

There are two situations in which a point becomes a _____ of a function of one variable. The first of which is that the value of the first derivative is equal to zero.

   a. Differentiation operator
   b. Multivariable calculus
   c. Total derivative
   d. Critical point

9. In calculus, a branch of mathematics, the _____ is a measurement of how a function changes when its input changes. Loosely speaking, a _____ can be thought of as how much a quantity is changing at some given point. For example, the _____ of the position (or distance) of a vehicle with respect to time is the instantaneous velocity (respectively, instantaneous speed) at which the vehicle is traveling.

The process of finding a _____ is called differentiation. The fundamental theorem of calculus states that differentiation is the reverse process to integration.

   a. Stationary phase approximation
   b. Semi-differentiability
   c. Bounded function
   d. Derivative

10. A real-valued function f defined on the real line is said to have a _____ point at the point $x^{>*}$, if there exists some $>\varepsilon > 0$, such that $f(x^{>*}) \geq f(x)$ when $|x >- x^{>*}| < >\varepsilon$. The value of the function at this point is called maximum of the function.

On a graph of a function, its local maxima will look like the tops of hills.

a. Local maximum
b. Standard part function
c. Test for Divergence
d. Racetrack principle

11. Similarly, a function has a _____ point at x^*, if $f(x^*) \leq f(x)$ when $|x - x^*| < \varepsilon$. The value of the function at this point is called minimum of the function.

On a graph of a function, its local minima will look like the bottoms of valleys.

a. Continuous function
b. Related rates
c. Local minimum
d. Complex analysis

12. In calculus, the _____ determines whether a given critical point of a function is a maximum, a minimum, or neither.

Suppose that f is a function and we want to determine if f has a maximum or minimum at x. If f is increasing to the left of x and decreasing to the right of x, then x is a local maximum of f.

a. Test for Divergence
b. Partial sum
c. Continuous function
d. First derivative test

13. In calculus, _____, was originally the use of expressions such as dx and dy and to represent 'infinitely small' (or infinitesimal) increments of quantities x and y, just as >Δx and >Δy represent finite increments of x and y respectively. So for y being a function of x, or

> [x] >

the derivative of y with respect to x, which later came to be viewed as

> [x] >

was, according to Leibniz, the quotient of an infinitesimal increment of y by an infinitesimal increment of x, or

$$\frac{dy}{dx},$$

where the right hand side is Lagrange's notation for the derivative of f at x.

Similarly, although mathematicians usually now view an integral

$$\int_a^b f(x)\,dx$$

as a limit

$$\lim_{\Delta x \to 0} \sum_i f(x_i)\,\Delta x,$$

where Δx is an interval containing x_i, Leibniz viewed it as the sum (the integral sign denoting summation) of infinitely many infinitesimal quantities f(x) dx.

  a. Smooth function
  b. Stationary point
  c. Time derivative
  d. Leibniz's notation

14. Let f be a differentiable function, and let f'(x) be its derivative. The derivative of f'(x) (if it has one) is written f''(x) and is called the _____ of f. Similarly, the derivative of a _____, if it exists, is written f'''(x) and is called the third derivative of f.
  a. Second derivative
  b. Stationary phase approximation
  c. Vertical asymptote
  d. Slant asymptote

15. Let f be a differentiable function, and let f'(x) be its derivative. The derivative of f'(x) (if it has one) is written f''(x) and is called the second derivative of f. Similarly, the derivative of a second derivative, if it exists, is written f'''(x) and is called the _____ of f.

a. Mountain pass theorem
b. Differential coefficient
c. Derivative
d. Third derivative

16. In physics, and more specifically kinematics, _____ is the change in velocity over time. Because velocity is a vector, it can change in two ways: a change in magnitude and/or a change in direction. In one dimension, _____ is the rate at which something speeds up or slows down.
   a. ACTRAN
   b. AUSM
   c. ALGOR
   d. Acceleration

17. In physics, _____ is defined as the rate of change of position. it is vector physical quantity; both speed and direction are required to define it. In the SI (metric) system, it is measured in meters per second: (m/s) or ms^{-1}.
   a. BIBO stability
   b. BDDC
   c. 15 theorem
   d. Velocity

18. In economics, the _____ functional form of production functions is widely used to represent the relationship of an output to inputs. It was proposed by Knut Wicksell (1851-1926), and tested against statistical evidence by Charles Cobb and Paul Douglas in 1900-1928.

For production, the function is

$$Y = AL^{\alpha}K^{\beta},$$

where:

- Y = total production (the monetary value of all goods produced in a year)
- L = labor input
- K = capital input
- A = total factor productivity
- α and β are the output elasticities of labor and capital, respectively. These values are constants determined by available technology.

Chapter 5. GRAPHS AND THE DERIVATIVE

Output elasticity measures the responsiveness of output to a change in levels of either labor or capital used in production, ceteris paribus. For example if α = 0.15, a 1% increase in labor would lead to approximately a 0.15% increase in output.

a. BDDC
b. 15 theorem
c. BIBO stability
d. Cobb-Douglas

19. In differential calculus, an inflection point, or _____ (or inflexion) is a point on a curve at which the curvature changes sign. The curve changes from being concave upwards (positive curvature) to concave downwards (negative curvature), or vice versa. If one imagines driving a vehicle along the curve, it is a point at which the steering-wheel is momentarily 'straight', being turned from left to right or vice versa.

a. Point of inflection
b. Derivative of a constant
c. Lin-Tsien equation
d. Logarithmic derivative

20. In calculus, a branch of mathematics, the _____ is a criterion often useful for determining whether a given stationary point of a function is a local maximum or a local minimum.

The test states: If the function f is twice differentiable at a stationary point x, meaning that $f'(x) = 0$, then:

- If $f''(x) < 0$ then f has a local maximum at x.
- If $f''(x) > 0$ then f has a local minimum at x.
- If $f''(x) = 0$, the _____ says nothing about the point x, has a possible inflection point.

In the last case, the function may have a local maximum or minimum there, but the function is sufficiently 'flat' that this is undetected by the second derivative. In this case one has to examine the third derivative. Such an example is f(x) = x^4.

a. Stationary point
b. Second derivative test
c. Symmetric derivative
d. Linearity of differentiation

21. An _____ of a real-valued function y = f(x) is a curve which describes the behavior of f as either x or y tends to infinity.

In other words, as one moves along the graph of f(x) in some direction, the distance between it and the _____ eventually becomes smaller than any distance that one may specify.

    a. AUSM
    b. ACTRAN
    c. ALGOR
    d. Asymptote

Chapter 6. APPLICATIONS OF THE DERIVATIVE

1. The largest and the smallest element of a set are called extreme values, absolute extrema, or extreme records.

   For a differentiable function f, if $f(x_0)$ is an _____ for the set of all values f(x), and if x_0 is in the interior of the domain of f, then x_0 is a critical point, by Fermat's theorem.

   In the case of a general partial order one should not confuse a least element (smaller than all other) and a minimal element (nothing is smaller.)

   a. Infinitesimal
   b. Extreme Value Theorem
   c. Integration by substitution
   d. Extreme value

2. In calculus, the _____ states that if a real-valued function f is continuous in the closed and bounded interval [a,b], then f must attain its maximum and minimum value, each at least once. That is, there exist numbers c and d in [a,b] such that:

   $$f(c) \geq f(x) \geq f(d) \quad \text{for all } x \in [a, b].$$

   A related theorem is the boundedness theorem which states that a continuous function f in the closed interval [a,b] is bounded on that interval. That is, there exist real numbers m and M such that:

   $$m \leq f(x) \leq M \quad \text{for all } x \in [a, b].$$

   The _____ enriches the boundedness theorem by saying that not only is the function bounded, but it also attains its least upper bound as its maximum and its greatest lower bound as its minimum.

   a. Integral of secant cubed
   b. Infinitesimal
   c. Uniform convergence
   d. Extreme value theorem

3. In metric topology and related fields of mathematics, a set U is called _____ if, intuitively speaking, starting from any point x in U one can move by a small amount in any direction and still be in the set U. In other words, the distance between any point x in U and the edge of U is always greater than zero.

   As an example, consider the _____ interval (0, 1) consisting of all real numbers x with 0 < x < 1. Here, the topology is the usual topology on the real line. We can look at this in two ways.

a. Open
b. AUSM
c. ACTRAN
d. ALGOR

4. In mathematics, the simplest case of _____ refers to the study of problems in which one seeks to minimize or maximize a real function by systematically choosing the values of real or integer variables from within an allowed set. This (a scalar real valued objective function) is actually a small subset of this field which comprises a large area of applied mathematics and generalizes to study of means to obtain 'best available' values of some objective function given a defined domain where the elaboration is on the types of functions and the conditions and nature of the objects in the problem domain.

The first _____ technique, which is known as steepest descent, goes back to Gauss.

a. ALGOR
b. AUSM
c. ACTRAN
d. Optimization

5. In a totally ordered set all elements are mutually comparable, so such a set can have at most one minimal element and at most one maximal element. Then, due to mutual comparability, the minimal element will also be the least element and the maximal element will also be the greatest element. Thus in a totally ordered set we can simply use the terms minimum and _____.

a. Leibniz rule
b. Racetrack principle
c. Maximum
d. Nth term

6. In calculus, a branch of mathematics, the _____ is a measurement of how a function changes when its input changes. Loosely speaking, a _____ can be thought of as how much a quantity is changing at some given point. For example, the _____ of the position (or distance) of a vehicle with respect to time is the instantaneous velocity (respectively, instantaneous speed) at which the vehicle is traveling.

The process of finding a _____ is called differentiation. The fundamental theorem of calculus states that differentiation is the reverse process to integration.

a. Semi-differentiability
b. Stationary phase approximation
c. Bounded function
d. Derivative

7. In calculus, a method called _____ can be applied to implicitly defined functions. This method is an application of the chain rule allowing one to calculate the derivative of a function given implicitly.

As explained in the introduction, y can be given as a function of x implicitly rather than explicitly. When we have an equation R (x,y) = 0, we may be able to solve it for y and then differentiate. However, sometimes it is simpler to differentiate R(x,y) with respect to x and then solve for dy / dx.

a. Ordinary differential equation
b. Implicit function
c. Implicit differentiation
d. Automatic differentiation

8. In mathematics, an _____ is a generalization for the concept of a function in which the dependent variable has not been given 'explicitly' in terms of the independent variable. To give a function f explicitly is to provide a prescription for determining the output value of the function y in terms of the input value x:

y = f(x.)

By contrast, the function is implicit if the value of y is obtained from x by solving an equation of the form:

R(x,y) = 0.

a. Implicit differentiation
b. Ordinary differential equation
c. Automatic differentiation
d. Implicit function

9. In physics, _____ is movement that changes the position of an object, as opposed to rotation. For example, according to Whittaker:

A _____ is the operation changing the positions of all points (x, y, z) of an object according to the formula

$$(x, y, z) \to (x + \Delta x, y + \Delta y, z + \Delta z)$$

where $(\Delta x, \Delta y, \Delta z)$ is the same vector for each point of the object. The _____ vector $(\Delta x, \Delta y, \Delta z)$ common to all points of the object describes a particular type of displacement of the object, usually called a linear displacement to distinguish it from displacements involving rotation, called angular displacements.

a. 15 theorem
b. BDDC
c. Translation
d. BIBO stability

10. In Geometry, the _____ is an algebraic curve defined by the equation

$$x^3 + y^3 - 3axy = 0$$

It forms a loop in the first quadrant with a double point at the origin and asymptote

$$x + y + a = 0$$

It is symmetrical about y = x.

a. Cochleoid
b. Curve
c. Folium of Descartes
d. Prolate cycloid

11. In geometry, the _____ or Gutschoven's curve is a two-dimensional algebraic curve resembling the Greek letter κ (kappa.)

Using the Cartesian coordinate system it can be expressed as:

$x^2(x^2 + y^2) = a^2 y^2$

or, using parametric equations:

$$\begin{aligned} x &= a\cos t \cot t \\ y &= a\cos t \end{aligned}$$

Chapter 6. APPLICATIONS OF THE DERIVATIVE

In polar coordinates its equation is even simpler:

r = atanθ

It has two vertical asymptotes at $x = \pm a$, shown as dashed blue lines in the figure at right.

The _____'s curvature:

$$\kappa(\theta) = \frac{8\left(3 - \sin^2\theta\right)\sin^4\theta}{a\left[\sin^2(2\theta) + 4\right]^{\frac{3}{2}}}$$

Tangential angle:

$$\phi(\theta) = -\arctan\left[\frac{1}{2}\sin(2\theta)\right]$$

The _____ was first studied by Gérard van Gutschoven around 1662.

a. Witch of Agnesi
b. Prolate cycloid
c. Kappa curve
d. Tractrix

12. In mathematics, a (topological) _____ is defined as follows: let I be an interval of real numbers (i.e. a non-empty connected subset of $\mathbb{R}$); then a _____ γ is a continuous mapping $\gamma : I \to X$, where X is a topological space. The _____ γ is said to be simple if it is injective, i.e. if for all x, y in I, we have $\gamma(x) = \gamma(y) \implies x = y$. If I is a closed bounded interval $[a, b]$, we also allow the possibility $\gamma(a) = \gamma(b)$ (this convention makes it possible to talk about closed simple _____.)
    a. Closed curve
    b. Tractrix
    c. Curve
    d. Prolate cycloid

13.

In differential calculus, _____ problems involve finding a rate that a quantity changes by relating the population of the earth. The rate of change is usually with respect to people who have died.

Chapter 6. APPLICATIONS OF THE DERIVATIVE

a. Standard part function
b. Mean Value Theorem
c. Visual Calculus
d. Related rates

14. In mathematics, a _____ is a function which preserves the given order. This concept first arose in calculus, and was later generalized to the more abstract setting of order theory.

In calculus, a function f defined on a subset of the real numbers with real values is called monotonic (also monotonically increasing or non-decreasing), if for all x and y such that x >≤ y one has f(x) >≤ f(y), so f preserves the order.

a. Pettis integral
b. Pseudo-differential operator
c. 15 theorem
d. Monotonic function

15. In infinitesimal calculus, a _____ is traditionally an infinitesimally small change in a variable. For example, if x is a variable, then a change in the value of x is often denoted Δx (or δx when this change is considered to be small.) The _____ dx represents such a change, but is infinitely small.

a. The Method of Mechanical Theorems
b. Local maximum
c. Dirichlet integral
d. Differential

16. A _____ is a statement of the meaning of a word or phrase. The term to be defined is known as the definiendum . The words which define it are known as the definiens .

a. BDDC
b. 15 theorem
c. BIBO stability
d. Definition

17. In mathematics, a _____ is an approximation of a general function using a linear function (more precisely, an affine function.)

Given a differentiable function f of one real variable, Taylor's theorem for n=1 states that

$$f(x) = f(a) + f'(a)(x-a) + R_2$$

where R_2 is the remainder term. The _____ is obtained by dropping the remainder:

$$f(x) \approx f(a) + f'(a)(x-a)$$

which is true for x close to a.

a. Linear approximation
b. Lin-Tsien equation
c. Point of inflection
d. Smooth function

Chapter 7. INTEGRATION

1. In calculus, an _____, primitive or indefinite integral of a function f is a function F whose derivative is equal to f, i.e., F >' = f. The process of solving for antiderivatives is antidifferentiation (or indefinite integration.) Antiderivatives are related to definite integrals through the fundamental theorem of calculus: the definite integral of a function over an interval is equal to the difference between the values of an _____ evaluated at the endpoints of the interval.
    a. Indefinite integral
    b. Integrand
    c. Order of integration
    d. Antiderivative

2. In infinitesimal calculus, a _____ is traditionally an infinitesimally small change in a variable. For example, if x is a variable, then a change in the value of x is often denoted Δx (or δx when this change is considered to be small.) The _____ dx represents such a change, but is infinitely small.
    a. Dirichlet integral
    b. Differential
    c. Local maximum
    d. The Method of Mechanical Theorems

3. _____, a field in mathematics, is the study of how functions change when their inputs change. The primary object of study in _____ is the derivative. A closely related notion is the differential.
    a. Slant asymptote
    b. Concave downwards
    c. Differential calculus
    d. Ramp function

4. _____ is a type of motion in which the velocity of an object changes equal amounts in equal time periods. An example of an object having _____ would be a ball rolling down a ramp. The object picks up velocity as it goes down the ramp with equal changes in time.
    a. ACTRAN
    b. AUSM
    c. ALGOR
    d. Uniform Acceleration

5. In calculus, the indefinite integral of a given function (i.e. the set of all antiderivatives of the function) is always written with a constant, the _____. This constant expresses an ambiguity inherent in the construction of antiderivatives. If a function f(x) is defined on an interval and F(x) is an antiderivative of f(x), then the set of all antiderivatives of f(x) is given by the functions F(x) + C, where C is an arbitrary constant.

a. Sum rule in integration
b. Disk integration
c. Nonelementary integral
d. Constant of integration

6. In calculus, an antiderivative, primitive or _____ of a function f is a function F whose derivative is equal to f, i.e., F ' = f. The process of solving for antiderivatives is antidifferentiation (or indefinite integration.) Antiderivatives are related to definite integrals through the fundamental theorem of calculus: the definite integral of a function over an interval is equal to the difference between the values of an antiderivative evaluated at the endpoints of the interval.

a. Integral test for convergence
b. Indefinite integral
c. Arc length
d. Integration by parts operator

7. Integration is an important concept in mathematics, specifically in the field of calculus and, more broadly, mathematical analysis. Given a function f of a real variable x and an interval [a, b] of the real line, the _____

$$\int_a^b f(x)\, dx,$$

is defined informally to be the net signed area of the region in the xy-plane bounded by the graph of f, the x-axis, and the vertical lines x = a and x = b.

The term '_____' may also refer to the notion of antiderivative, a function F whose derivative is the given function f.

a. Integral test for convergence
b. Integral
c. Indefinite integral
d. Integrand

8. If a function has an integral, it is said to be integrable. The function for which the integral is calculated is called the _____. The region over which a function is being integrated is called the domain of integration.

a. Integrand
b. Integration by parts
c. Order of integration
d. Integral test for convergence

9. This article will state and prove the _____ for differentiation, and then use it to prove these two formulas.

The _____ for differentiation states that for every natural number n, the derivative of $f(x) = x^n$ is $f'(x) = nx^{n-1}$, that is,

$$(x^n)' = nx^{n-1}.$$

The _____ for integration

$$\int x^n \, dx = \frac{x^{n+1}}{n+1} + C$$

for natural n is then an easy consequence. One just needs to take the derivative of this equality and use the _____ and linearity of differentiation on the right-hand side.

a. Leibniz rule
b. Power rule
c. Test for Divergence
d. Functional integration

10. In calculus, a branch of mathematics, the _____ is a measurement of how a function changes when its input changes. Loosely speaking, a _____ can be thought of as how much a quantity is changing at some given point. For example, the _____ of the position (or distance) of a vehicle with respect to time is the instantaneous velocity (respectively, instantaneous speed) at which the vehicle is traveling.

The process of finding a _____ is called differentiation. The fundamental theorem of calculus states that differentiation is the reverse process to integration.

a. Bounded function
b. Stationary phase approximation
c. Semi-differentiability
d. Derivative

11. In physics, _____ is movement that changes the position of an object, as opposed to rotation. For example, according to Whittaker:

Chapter 7. INTEGRATION

A _____ is the operation changing the positions of all points (x, y, z) of an object according to the formula

$$(x, y, z) \rightarrow (x + \Delta x, y + \Delta y, z + \Delta z)$$

where $(\Delta x, \Delta y, \Delta z)$ is the same vector for each point of the object. The _____ vector $(\Delta x, \Delta y, \Delta z)$ common to all points of the object describes a particular type of displacement of the object, usually called a linear displacement to distinguish it from displacements involving rotation, called angular displacements.

a. BDDC
b. Translation
c. BIBO stability
d. 15 theorem

12. In calculus, the _____ allows you to take constants outside a derivative and concentrate on differentiating the function of x itself. This is a part of the linearity of differentiation.

Suppose you have a function

$$g(x) = k \cdot f(x).$$

where k is a constant.

Use the formula for differentiation from first principles to obtain:

$$g'(x) = \lim_{h \to 0} \frac{g(x+h) - g(x)}{h}$$
$$g'(x) = \lim_{h \to 0} \frac{k \cdot f(x+h) - k \cdot f(x)}{h}$$
$$g'(x) = \lim_{h \to 0} \frac{k(f(x+h) - f(x))}{h}$$
$$g'(x) = k \lim_{h \to 0} \frac{f(x+h) - f(x)}{h} \quad (*)$$
$$g'(x) = k \cdot f'(x).$$

This is the statement of the _____, in Lagrange's notation for differentiation.

Chapter 7. INTEGRATION

a. Quotient Rule
b. Constant factor rule in differentiation
c. Reciprocal Rule
d. Product rule

13. The _____ is a function in mathematics. The application of this function to a value x is written as exp(x). Equivalently, this can be written in the form e^x, where e is a mathematical constant, the base of the natural logarithm, which equals approximately 2.718281828, and is also known as Euler's number.

a. ACTRAN
b. Area hyperbolic functions
c. Integral part
d. Exponential function

14. In calculus, _____ is a tool for finding antiderivatives and integrals. Using the fundamental theorem of calculus often requires finding an antiderivative. For this and other reasons, _____ is a relatively important tool for mathematicians.

a. Odd function
b. Integral of secant cubed
c. Extreme value
d. Integration by substitution

15. A _____ officer is an officer of high military rank. The term or equivalent is used by nearly every country in the world. _____ can be used as a generic term for all grades of _____ officer, or it can specifically refer to a single rank that is just called _____.

a. 15 theorem
b. BDDC
c. BIBO stability
d. General

16. In mathematics, a (topological) _____ is defined as follows: let I be an interval of real numbers (i.e. a non-empty connected subset of $\mathbb{R}$); then a _____ γ is a continuous mapping $\gamma : I \to X$, where X is a topological space. The _____ γ is said to be simple if it is injective, i.e. if for all x, y in I, we have $\gamma(x) = \gamma(y) \implies x = y$. If I is a closed bounded interval $[a, b]$, we also allow the possibility $\gamma(a) = \gamma(b)$ (this convention makes it possible to talk about closed simple _____.)

a. Curve
b. Closed curve
c. Prolate cycloid
d. Tractrix

17. In mathematics, the _____ is a way to approximately calculate the definite integral

$$\int_a^b f(x)\,dx.$$

The _____ works by approximating the region under the graph of the function f by a trapezoid and calculating its area. It follows that

$$\int_a^b f(x)\,dx \approx (b-a)\frac{f(a)+f(b)}{2}.$$

To calculate this integral more accurately, one first splits the interval of integration [a,b] into n smaller subintervals, and then applies the _____ on each of them. One obtains the composite _____:

$$\int_a^b f(x)\,dx \approx \frac{b-a}{n}\left[\frac{f(a)+f(b)}{2} + \sum_{k=1}^{n-1} f\left(a+k\frac{b-a}{n}\right)\right].$$

This can alternatively be written as:

$$\int_a^b f(x)\,dx \approx \frac{b-a}{2n}\left(f(x_0)+2f(x_1)+2f(x_2)+\cdots+2f(x_{n-1})+f(x_n)\right)$$

where

$$x_k = a + k\frac{b-a}{n}, \text{ for } k = 0, 1, \ldots, n$$

(one can also use a non-uniform grid.)

a. Trapezoidal rule
b. BIBO stability
c. 15 theorem
d. BDDC

Chapter 7. INTEGRATION

18. _____ is the addition of a set of numbers; the result is their sum or total. An interim or present total of a _____ process is termed the running total. The 'numbers' to be summed may be natural numbers, complex numbers, matrices, or still more complicated objects.
   a. 15 theorem
   b. BDDC
   c. BIBO stability
   d. Summation

19. In the branch of mathematics known as real analysis, the _____, created by Bernhard Riemann, was the first rigorous definition of the integral of a function on an interval. While the _____ is unsuitable for many theoretical purposes, it is one of the easiest integrals to define. Some of these technical deficiencies can be remedied by the Riemann-Stieltjes integral, and most of them disappear in the Lebesgue integral.
   a. Lebesgue integration
   b. Regulated integral
   c. Skorokhod integral
   d. Riemann integral

20. In mathematics, a _____ is a method for approximating the total area underneath a curve on a graph, otherwise known as an integral. It may also be used to define the integration operation.

    Consider a function $f: D \to \mathbf{R}$, where D is a subset of the real numbers $\mathbf{R}$, and let $I = [a, b]$ be a closed interval contained in D. A finite set of points $\{x_0, x_1, x_2, \ldots x_n\}$ such that $a = x_0 < x_1 < x_2 \ldots < x_n = b$ creates a partition

    $$P = \{[x_0, x_1), [x_1, x_2), \ldots [x_{n-1}, x_n]\}$$

    of I.

   a. Riemann sum
   b. Solid of revolution
   c. Risch algorithm
   d. Signed measure

21. In mathematics, the concept of a '_____' is used to describe the behavior of a function as its argument or input either 'gets close' to some point, or as the argument becomes arbitrarily large; or the behavior of a sequence's elements as their index increases indefinitely. Limits are used in calculus and other branches of mathematical analysis to define derivatives and continuity.

    In formulas, _____ is usually abbreviated as lim

a. 15 theorem
b. BDDC
c. BIBO stability
d. Limit

22. In mathematics, the simplest case of _____ refers to the study of problems in which one seeks to minimize or maximize a real function by systematically choosing the values of real or integer variables from within an allowed set. This (a scalar real valued objective function) is actually a small subset of this field which comprises a large area of applied mathematics and generalizes to study of means to obtain 'best available' values of some objective function given a defined domain where the elaboration is on the types of functions and the conditions and nature of the objects in the problem domain.

The first _____ technique, which is known as steepest descent, goes back to Gauss.

a. ACTRAN
b. Optimization
c. AUSM
d. ALGOR

23. The _____ specifies the relationship between the two central operations of calculus, differentiation and integration.

The first part of the theorem, sometimes called the first _____, shows that an indefinite integration can be reversed by a differentiation.

The second part, sometimes called the second _____, allows one to compute the definite integral of a function by using any one of its infinitely many antiderivatives.

a. Limits of integration
b. Fundamental Theorem of Calculus
c. Leibniz formula
d. Periodic function

24. _____ is any physical or virtual entity that is owned by an individual or jointly by a group of individuals. An owner of _____ has the right to consume, sell, rent, mortgage, transfer and exchange his or her _____. Important widely-recognized types of _____ include real _____, personal _____ (other physical possessions), and intellectual _____ (rights over artistic creations, inventions, etc.), although the latter is not always as widely recognized or enforced.

Chapter 7. INTEGRATION

a. Property
b. 15 theorem
c. BIBO stability
d. BDDC

25. In numerical analysis, _____ constitutes a broad family of algorithms for calculating the numerical value of a definite integral, and by extension, the term is also sometimes used to describe the numerical solution of differential equations The term numerical quadrature is more or less a synonym for _____, especially as applied to one-dimensional integrals.
    a. Meshfree methods
    b. Multigrid method
    c. Galerkin methods
    d. Numerical integration

26. _____ is the study of algorithms for the problems of continuous mathematics (as distinguished from discrete mathematics.)

One of the earliest mathematical writings is the Babylonian tablet YBC 7289, which gives a sexagesimal numerical approximation of $\sqrt{2}$, the length of the diagonal in a unit square. Being able to compute the sides of a triangle (and hence, being able to compute square roots) is extremely important, for instance, in carpentry and construction.

   a. Numerical analysis
   b. 15 theorem
   c. BDDC
   d. BIBO stability

27. A _____ is a statement of the meaning of a word or phrase. The term to be defined is known as the definiendum . The words which define it are known as the definiens .
    a. 15 theorem
    b. BIBO stability
    c. BDDC
    d. Definition

28. In calculus, an _____ is the limit of a definite integral as an endpoint of the interval of integration approaches either a specified real number or ∞ or −∞ or, in some cases, as both endpoints approach limits.

Specifically, an _____ is a limit of the form

$$\lim_{b\to\infty} \int_a^b f(x)\,dx, \qquad \lim_{a\to-\infty} \int_a^b f(x)\,dx,$$

or of the form

$$\lim_{c\to b^-} \int_a^c f(x)\,dx, \qquad \lim_{c\to a^+} \int_c^b f(x)\,dx,$$

in which one takes a limit in one or the other (or sometimes both) endpoints. Improper integrals may also occur at an interior point of the domain of integration, or at multiple such points.

a. ALGOR
b. ACTRAN
c. AUSM
d. Improper integral

Chapter 8. FURTHER TECHNIQUES AND APPLICATIONS OF INTEGRATION

1. In calculus, and more generally in mathematical analysis, _____ is a rule that transforms the integral of products of functions into other, hopefully simpler, integrals. The rule arises from the product rule of differentiation.

If u = f(x), v = g(x), and the differentials du = f '(x) dx and dv = g'(x) dx; then in its simplest form the product rule is:

$$\int u\,dv = uv - \int v\,du.$$

Suppose f(x) and g(x) are two continuously differentiable functions.

 a. Integrand
 b. Integration by parametric derivatives
 c. Integration by parts
 d. Arc length

2. _____ generally conveys two primary meanings. The first is an imprecise sense of harmonious or aesthetically-pleasing proportionality and balance; such that it reflects beauty or perfection. The second meaning is a precise and well-defined concept of balance or 'patterned self-similarity' that can be demonstrated or proved according to the rules of a formal system: by geometry, through physics or otherwise.
 a. BIBO stability
 b. BDDC
 c. 15 theorem
 d. Symmetry

3. In mathematics, the _____ is a conic section, the intersection of a right circular conical surface and a plane parallel to a generating straight line of that surface. Given a point (the focus) and a line (the directrix) that lie in a plane, the locus of points in that plane that are equidistant to them is a _____.

A particular case arises when the plane is tangent to the conical surface of a circle.

 a. Parabola
 b. BIBO stability
 c. 15 theorem
 d. BDDC

4. In mathematics, engineering, and manufacturing, a _____ is a solid figure obtained by rotating a plane curve around some straight line (the axis) that lies on the same plane.

Chapter 8. FURTHER TECHNIQUES AND APPLICATIONS OF INTEGRATION

Assuming that the curve does not cross the axis, the solid's volume is equal to the length of the circle described by the figure's centroid, times the figure's area (Pappus's second centroid Theorem.)

Rotating a curve

A representative disk is a three-dimensional volume element of a _____.

- a. Trigonometric substitution
- b. Riemann sum
- c. Solid of revolution
- d. Surface of revolution

5. In physics, _____ is movement that changes the position of an object, as opposed to rotation. For example, according to Whittaker:

A _____ is the operation changing the positions of all points (x, y, z) of an object according to the formula

$$(x, y, z) \rightarrow (x + \Delta x, y + \Delta y, z + \Delta z)$$

where $(\Delta x, \Delta y, \Delta z)$ is the same vector for each point of the object. The _____ vector $(\Delta x, \Delta y, \Delta z)$ common to all points of the object describes a particular type of displacement of the object, usually called a linear displacement to distinguish it from displacements involving rotation, called angular displacements.

- a. 15 theorem
- b. BIBO stability
- c. Translation
- d. BDDC

6. The _____ of any solid, liquid, plasma, vacuum or theoretical object is how much three-dimensional space it occupies, often quantified numerically. One-dimensional figures (such as lines) and two-dimensional shapes (such as squares) are assigned zero _____ in the three-dimensional space. _____ is commonly presented in units such as mL or cm^3 (milliliters or cubic centimeters.)
- a. Dirac equation
- b. Vector potential
- c. Klein-Gordon equation
- d. Volume

Chapter 8. FURTHER TECHNIQUES AND APPLICATIONS OF INTEGRATION

7. _____ was a German mathematician, astronomer and astrologer, and key figure in the 17th century scientific revolution. He is best known for his eponymous laws of planetary motion, codified by later astronomers based on his works Astronomia nova, Harmonices Mundi, and Epitome of Copernican Astrononomy. They also provided one of the foundations for Isaac Newton's theory of universal gravitation.
   a. Johannes Kepler
   b. Robin K. Bullough
   c. Niels Henrik David Bohr
   d. MÄ dhava of Sangamagrama

8. In calculus, an _____ is the limit of a definite integral as an endpoint of the interval of integration approaches either a specified real number or ∞ or −∞ or, in some cases, as both endpoints approach limits.

   Specifically, an _____ is a limit of the form

   $$\lim_{b \to \infty} \int_a^b f(x)\,dx, \qquad \lim_{a \to -\infty} \int_a^b f(x)\,dx,$$

   or of the form

   $$\lim_{c \to b^-} \int_a^c f(x)\,dx, \qquad \lim_{c \to a^+} \int_c^b f(x)\,dx,$$

   in which one takes a limit in one or the other (or sometimes both) endpoints . Improper integrals may also occur at an interior point of the domain of integration, or at multiple such points.

   a. AUSM
   b. ACTRAN
   c. Improper integral
   d. ALGOR

9. Integration is an important concept in mathematics, specifically in the field of calculus and, more broadly, mathematical analysis. Given a function f of a real variable x and an interval [a, b] of the real line, the _____

   $$\int_a^b f(x)\,dx,$$

   is defined informally to be the net signed area of the region in the xy-plane bounded by the graph of f, the x-axis, and the vertical lines x = a and x = b.

Chapter 8. FURTHER TECHNIQUES AND APPLICATIONS OF INTEGRATION

The term '_____' may also refer to the notion of antiderivative, a function F whose derivative is the given function f.

a. Integrand
b. Indefinite integral
c. Integral
d. Integral test for convergence

10. _____ is any physical or virtual entity that is owned by an individual or jointly by a group of individuals. An owner of _____ has the right to consume, sell, rent, mortgage, transfer and exchange his or her _____. Important widely-recognized types of _____ include real _____, personal _____ (other physical possessions), and intellectual _____ (rights over artistic creations, inventions, etc.), although the latter is not always as widely recognized or enforced.

a. BDDC
b. Property
c. 15 theorem
d. BIBO stability

11. In mathematics, a (topological) _____ is defined as follows: let I be an interval of real numbers (i.e. a non-empty connected subset of $\mathbb{R}$); then a _____ γ is a continuous mapping $\gamma : I \to X$, where X is a topological space. The _____ γ is said to be simple if it is injective, i.e. if for all x, y in I, we have $\gamma(x) = \gamma(y) \implies x = y$. If I is a closed bounded interval $[a, b]$, we also allow the possibility $\gamma(a) = \gamma(b)$ (this convention makes it possible to talk about closed simple _____.)

a. Prolate cycloid
b. Curve
c. Tractrix
d. Closed curve

12. A _____ is a statement of the meaning of a word or phrase. The term to be defined is known as the definiendum. The words which define it are known as the definiens.

a. BDDC
b. 15 theorem
c. BIBO stability
d. Definition

13. _____ is the extension of calculus in one variable to calculus in several variables: the functions which are differentiated and integrated involve several variables rather than one variable.

Chapter 8. FURTHER TECHNIQUES AND APPLICATIONS OF INTEGRATION

A study of limits and continuity in multiple dimensions yields many counter-intuitive and pathological results not demonstrated by single-variable functions. There exist, for example, scalar functions of two variables having points in their domain which, when approached along any arbitrary line, give a particular limit, yet give a different limit when approached along a parabola.

a. Scalar field
b. Laplace invariant
c. Total derivative
d. Multivariable calculus

14. In elementary algebra, a _____ is a polynomial with two terms--the sum of two monomials--often bound by parenthesis or brackets when operated upon. It is the simplest kind of polynomial other than monomials.

- The _____ $a^2 - b^2$ can be factored as the product of two other binomials:

    $a^2 - b^2 = (a + b)(a - b.)$

    This is a special case of the more general formula:

    $$a^{n+1} - b^{n+1} = (a - b) \sum_{k=0}^{n} a^k b^{n-k}$$

- The product of a pair of linear binomials (ax + b) and (cx + d) is:

    $(ax + b)(cx + d) = acx^2 + axd + bcx + bd.$

- A _____ raised to the nth power, represented as

    $(a + b)^n$

    can be expanded by means of the _____ theorem or, equivalently, using Pascal's triangle. Taking a simple example, the perfect square _____ $(p + q)^2$ can be found by squaring the first digit, adding twice the product of the first and second digit and finally adding the square of the second digit, to give $p^2 + 2pq + q^2$.

a. Partial fractions
b. Multinomial theorem
c. Completing the square
d. Binomial

15. In infinitesimal calculus, a _____ is traditionally an infinitesimally small change in a variable. For example, if x is a variable, then a change in the value of x is often denoted Δx (or δx when this change is considered to be small.) The _____ dx represents such a change, but is infinitely small.

a. Dirichlet integral
b. Differential
c. The Method of Mechanical Theorems
d. Local maximum

Chapter 9. MULTIVARIABLE CALCULUS

1. The terms '_____' and 'independent variable' are used in similar but subtly different ways in mathematics and statistics as part of the standard terminology in those subjects. They are used to distinguish between two types of quantities being considered, separating them into those available at the start of a process and those being created by it, where the latter (dependent variables) are dependent on the former (independent variables.)

   In traditional calculus, a function is defined as a relation between two terms called variables because their values vary.

   a. BIBO stability
   b. BDDC
   c. 15 theorem
   d. Dependent variable

2. The terms 'dependent variable' and '_____' are used in similar but subtly different ways in mathematics and statistics as part of the standard terminology in those subjects. They are used to distinguish between two types of quantities being considered, separating them into those available at the start of a process and those being created by it, where the latter (dependent variables) are dependent on the former (independent variables.)

   In traditional calculus, a function is defined as a relation between two terms called variables because their values vary.

   a. Independent variable
   b. ACTRAN
   c. ALGOR
   d. AUSM

3. In mathematics, the _____ (or replacement set) of a given function is the set of 'input' values for which the function is defined. For instance, the _____ of cosine would be all real numbers, while the _____ of the square root would be only numbers greater than or equal to 0 (ignoring complex numbers in both cases.) In a representation of a function in a xy Cartesian coordinate system, the _____ is represented on the x axis (or abscissa.)
   a. 15 theorem
   b. BIBO stability
   c. Domain
   d. BDDC

4. In mathematics, the _____ of a function is the set of all 'output' values produced by that function. Sometimes it is called the image, or more precisely, the image of the domain of the function. If a function is a surjection then its _____ is equal to its codomain.

Chapter 9. MULTIVARIABLE CALCULUS

a. Surjective
b. Range
c. Constant function
d. Piecewise-defined function

5. In mathematics, a (topological) _____ is defined as follows: let I be an interval of real numbers (i.e. a non-empty connected subset of $\mathbb{R}$); then a _____ γ is a continuous mapping $\gamma : I \to X$, where X is a topological space. The _____ γ is said to be simple if it is injective, i.e. if for all x, y in I, we have $\gamma(x) = \gamma(y) \implies x = y$. If I is a closed bounded interval $[a, b]$, we also allow the possibility $\gamma(a) = \gamma(b)$ (this convention makes it possible to talk about closed simple _____.)

a. Closed curve
b. Prolate cycloid
c. Curve
d. Tractrix

6. When the number of variables is two, this is a _____, if it is three this is a level surface, and for higher values of n the level set is a level hypersurface.

More specifically, a _____ is the set of all real-valued roots of an equation in two variables x_1 and x_2. A level surface is the set of all real-valued roots of an equation in three variables x_1, x_2 and x_3.

a. Partial derivative
b. Multipole moment
c. Scalar field
d. Level curve

7. In mathematics, a _____ is a quadric surface of special kind. There are two kinds of paraboloids: elliptic and hyperbolic. The elliptic _____ is shaped like an oval cup and can have a maximum or minimum point.

a. Hyperbolic paraboloid
b. Torus
c. Paraboloid
d. PDE surfaces

8. In economics, the _____ functional form of production functions is widely used to represent the relationship of an output to inputs. It was proposed by Knut Wicksell (1851-1926), and tested against statistical evidence by Charles Cobb and Paul Douglas in 1900-1928.

For production, the function is

$$Y = AL^\alpha K^\beta,$$

where:

- Y = total production (the monetary value of all goods produced in a year)
- L = labor input
- K = capital input
- A = total factor productivity
- α and β are the output elasticities of labor and capital, respectively. These values are constants determined by available technology.

Output elasticity measures the responsiveness of output to a change in levels of either labor or capital used in production, ceteris paribus. For example if α = 0.15, a 1% increase in labor would lead to approximately a 0.15% increase in output.

a. 15 theorem
b. BIBO stability
c. Cobb-Douglas
d. BDDC

9. An _____ is a type of quadric surface that is a higher dimensional analogue of an ellipse. The equation of a standard axis-aligned _____ body in an xyz-Cartesian coordinate system is

$$\frac{x^2}{a^2} + \frac{y^2}{b^2} + \frac{z^2}{c^2} = 1$$

where a and b are the equatorial radii (along the x and y axes) and c is the polar radius (along the z-axis), all of which are fixed positive real numbers determining the shape of the _____.

More generally, a not-necessarily-axis-aligned _____ is defined by the equation

$$\mathbf{x}^T A \mathbf{x} = 1$$

where A is a symmetric positive definite matrix and x is a vector.

Chapter 9. MULTIVARIABLE CALCULUS

a. AUSM
b. ALGOR
c. ACTRAN
d. Ellipsoid

10. The _____ is a doubly ruled surface shaped like a saddle. In a suitable coordinate system, it can be represented by the equation

$$z = \frac{x^2}{a^2} - \frac{y^2}{b^2}.$$

This is a _____ that opens up along the x-axis and down along the y-axis.

Paraboloid of revolution

With a = b an elliptic paraboloid is a paraboloid of revolution: a surface obtained by revolving a parabola around its axis.

a. Torus
b. Parametric surface
c. Paraboloid
d. Hyperbolic paraboloid

11. In calculus, _____, was originally the use of expressions such as dx and dy and to represent 'infinitely small' (or infinitesimal) increments of quantities x and y, just as >Δx and >Δy represent finite increments of x and y respectively. So for y being a function of x, or

the derivative of y with respect to x, which later came to be viewed as

was, according to Leibniz, the quotient of an infinitesimal increment of y by an infinitesimal increment of x, or

where the right hand side is Lagrange's notation for the derivative of f at x.

Similarly, although mathematicians usually now view an integral

$$\int f(x)\,dx$$

as a limit

$$\lim \sum f(x_i)\,\Delta x$$

where Δx is an interval containing x_i, Leibniz viewed it as the sum (the integral sign denoting summation) of infinitely many infinitesimal quantities f(x) dx.

   a. Stationary point
   b. Smooth function
   c. Time derivative
   d. Leibniz's notation

12. In mathematics, a _____ of a function of several variables is its derivative with respect to one of those variables with the others held constant (as opposed to the total derivative, in which all variables are allowed to vary.) Partial derivatives are useful in vector calculus and differential geometry.

The _____ of a function f with respect to the variable x is written as f'_x, $\partial_x f$, or $\partial f/\partial x$.

   a. Level curve
   b. Differentiation operator
   c. Jacobian
   d. Partial derivative

13. In calculus, a branch of mathematics, the _____ is a measurement of how a function changes when its input changes. Loosely speaking, a _____ can be thought of as how much a quantity is changing at some given point. For example, the _____ of the position (or distance) of a vehicle with respect to time is the instantaneous velocity (respectively, instantaneous speed) at which the vehicle is traveling.

The process of finding a _____ is called differentiation. The fundamental theorem of calculus states that differentiation is the reverse process to integration.

Chapter 9. MULTIVARIABLE CALCULUS

a. Stationary phase approximation
b. Bounded function
c. Semi-differentiability
d. Derivative

14. A _____ is a statement of the meaning of a word or phrase. The term to be defined is known as the definiendum. The words which define it are known as the definiens.
   a. Definition
   b. BDDC
   c. BIBO stability
   d. 15 theorem

15. In mathematics, _____ and minima, known collectively as extrema, are the largest value (maximum) or smallest value (minimum), that a function takes in a point either within a given neighbourhood (local extremum) or on the function domain in its entirety (global extremum.)

Throughout, a point refers to an input (x), while a value refers to an output (y): one distinguishing between the maximum value and the point (or points) at which it occurs.

A real-valued function f defined on the real line is said to have a local maximum point at the point x^*, if there exists some $\varepsilon > 0$, such that $f(x^*) \geq f(x)$ when $|x - x^*| < \varepsilon$.

   a. Leibniz formula
   b. Related rates
   c. Racetrack principle
   d. Maxima

16. In a totally ordered set all elements are mutually comparable, so such a set can have at most one minimal element and at most one maximal element. Then, due to mutual comparability, the minimal element will also be the least element and the maximal element will also be the greatest element. Thus in a totally ordered set we can simply use the terms minimum and _____.

   a. Racetrack principle
   b. Leibniz rule
   c. Nth term
   d. Maximum

Chapter 9. MULTIVARIABLE CALCULUS

17. In a totally ordered set all elements are mutually comparable, so such a set can have at most one minimal element and at most one maximal element. Then, due to mutual comparability, the minimal element will also be the least element and the maximal element will also be the greatest element. Thus in a totally ordered set we can simply use the terms _____ and maximum.
    a. Minimum
    b. Nth term
    c. Ghosts of departed quantities
    d. Maximum

18. In mathematics, a _____ (or critical number) is a point on the domain of a function where:

    - one dimension: the derivative (or slope of the line when visualized) is equal to zero or a point where the function ceases to be differentiable.
    - in general: there are two distinct concepts: either the derivative (Jacobian) vanishes, or it is not of full rank (or, in either case, the function is not differentiable); these agree in one dimension.

    Note that in one dimension, a critical value or critical number x of function f is the domain element at which the derivative is zero or undefined, whereas the associated ordered pair (x, y) is the _____. In higher dimensions a critical value is in the range whereas a _____ is in the domain.

    There are two situations in which a point becomes a _____ of a function of one variable. The first of which is that the value of the first derivative is equal to zero.

    a. Multivariable calculus
    b. Total derivative
    c. Differentiation operator
    d. Critical point

19. In mathematics, a _____ is a point in the domain of a function of two variables which is a stationary point but not a local extremum. At such a point, in general, the surface resembles a saddle that curves up in one direction, and curves down in a different direction (like a mountain pass.) In terms of contour lines, a _____ can be recognized, in general, by a contour that appears to intersect itself.
    a. BDDC
    b. Saddle point
    c. BIBO stability
    d. 15 theorem

20. _____ is the addition of a set of numbers; the result is their sum or total. An interim or present total of a _____ process is termed the running total. The 'numbers' to be summed may be natural numbers, complex numbers, matrices, or still more complicated objects.

a. 15 theorem
b. BDDC
c. BIBO stability
d. Summation

21. In mathematical optimization, the method of Lagrange multipliers provides a strategy for finding the maximum/minimum of a function subject to constraints.

For example , consider the optimization problem

$$\begin{aligned} \text{maximize } & f(x,y) \\ \text{subject to } & g(x,y) = c. \end{aligned}$$

We introduce a new variable (λ) called a _____, and study the Lagrange function defined by

$$\Lambda(x,y,\lambda) = f(x,y) - \lambda\Big(g(x,y) - c\Big).$$

If (x,y)â‰ is a maximum for the original constrained problem, then there exists a λ such that (x,y,λ)â‰ is a stationary point for the Lagrange function (stationary points are those points where the partial derivatives of Λ are zero.) However, not all stationary points yield a solution of the original problem.

a. BDDC
b. BIBO stability
c. 15 theorem
d. Lagrange multiplier

22. In infinitesimal calculus, a _____ is traditionally an infinitesimally small change in a variable. For example, if x is a variable, then a change in the value of x is often denoted Δx (or δx when this change is considered to be small.) The _____ dx represents such a change, but is infinitely small.
a. The Method of Mechanical Theorems
b. Dirichlet integral
c. Local maximum
d. Differential

Chapter 9. MULTIVARIABLE CALCULUS

23. Just as the definite integral of a positive function of one variable represents the area of the region between the graph of the function and the x-axis, the _____ of a positive function of two variables represents the volume of the region between the surface defined by the function (on the three dimensional Cartesian plane where z = f(x,y)) and the plane which contains its domain. (Note that the same volume can be obtained via the triple integral -- the integral of a function in three variables -- of the constant function f(x, y, z) = 1 over the above-mentioned region between the surface and the plane.) If there are more variables, a multiple integral will yield hypervolumes of multi-dimensional functions.
   a. Constant of integration
   b. Trigonometric substitution
   c. Risch algorithm
   d. Double integral

24. Integration is an important concept in mathematics, specifically in the field of calculus and, more broadly, mathematical analysis. Given a function f of a real variable x and an interval [a, b] of the real line, the _____

$$\int_a^b f(x)\,dx,$$

is defined informally to be the net signed area of the region in the xy-plane bounded by the graph of f, the x-axis, and the vertical lines x = a and x = b.

The term '_____' may also refer to the notion of antiderivative, a function F whose derivative is the given function f.

   a. Indefinite integral
   b. Integral test for convergence
   c. Integrand
   d. Integral

25. If a function has an integral, it is said to be integrable. The function for which the integral is calculated is called the _____. The region over which a function is being integrated is called the domain of integration.
   a. Order of integration
   b. Integrand
   c. Integration by parts
   d. Integral test for convergence

26. In physics, _____ is movement that changes the position of an object, as opposed to rotation. For example, according to Whittaker:

Chapter 9. MULTIVARIABLE CALCULUS

A _____ is the operation changing the positions of all points (x, y, z) of an object according to the formula

$$(x,y,z) \rightarrow (x + \Delta x, y + \Delta y, z + \Delta z)$$

where $(\Delta x, \Delta y, \Delta z)$ is the same vector for each point of the object. The _____ vector $(\Delta x, \Delta y, \Delta z)$ common to all points of the object describes a particular type of displacement of the object, usually called a linear displacement to distinguish it from displacements involving rotation, called angular displacements.

a. Translation
b. BIBO stability
c. 15 theorem
d. BDDC

27. The _____ of any solid, liquid, plasma, vacuum or theoretical object is how much three-dimensional space it occupies, often quantified numerically. One-dimensional figures (such as lines) and two-dimensional shapes (such as squares) are assigned zero _____ in the three-dimensional space. _____ is commonly presented in units such as mL or cm^3 (milliliters or cubic centimeters.)

a. Vector potential
b. Dirac equation
c. Klein-Gordon equation
d. Volume

28. In mathematics, the concept of a '_____' is used to describe the behavior of a function as its argument or input either 'gets close' to some point, or as the argument becomes arbitrarily large; or the behavior of a sequence's elements as their index increases indefinitely. Limits are used in calculus and other branches of mathematical analysis to define derivatives and continuity.

In formulas, _____ is usually abbreviated as lim

a. BDDC
b. 15 theorem
c. BIBO stability
d. Limit

29. In calculus and mathematical analysis the _____ of the integral

$$\int_a^b f(x)\,dx$$

of a Riemann integrable function f defined on a closed and bounded interval [a, b] are the real numbers a and b.

_____ can also be defined for improper integrals, with the _____ of both

$$\lim_{z \to a+} \int_z^b f(x)\,dx$$

and

$$\lim_{z \to b-} \int_a^z f(x)\,dx$$

again being a and b. For an improper integral

$$\int_a^\infty f(x)\,dx$$

or

$$\int_{-\infty}^b f(x)\,dx$$

the _____ are a and ∞, or −∞ and b, respectively.

a. Test for Divergence
b. Maxima
c. Differential
d. Limits of Integration

ANSWER KEY

Chapter 1
1. d   2. b   3. b   4. b   5. a   6. b   7. d   8. b   9. d   10. d
11. d   12. c   13. a   14. d   15. d   16. a   17. d   18. d   19. d   20. d
21. d   22. d

Chapter 2
1. c   2. b   3. d   4. b   5. d   6. c   7. d   8. d   9. a   10. d
11. b   12. a   13. d   14. d   15. d   16. d   17. d   18. d   19. c   20. d
21. b   22. b   23. c   24. d   25. b   26. a   27. c   28. d   29. b

Chapter 3
1. d   2. d   3. d   4. d   5. d   6. a   7. d   8. d   9. d   10. c
11. c   12. d   13. d   14. d   15. a   16. d   17. d   18. c   19. b   20. d
21. d

Chapter 4
1. d   2. d   3. d   4. d   5. a   6. d   7. c   8. a   9. d   10. d
11. d   12. a   13. b   14. d   15. b   16. d   17. b

Chapter 5
1. d   2. d   3. d   4. d   5. d   6. d   7. d   8. d   9. d   10. a
11. c   12. d   13. d   14. a   15. d   16. d   17. d   18. d   19. a   20. b
21. d

Chapter 6
1. d   2. d   3. a   4. d   5. c   6. d   7. c   8. d   9. c   10. c
11. c   12. c   13. d   14. d   15. d   16. d   17. a

Chapter 7
1. d   2. b   3. c   4. d   5. d   6. b   7. b   8. a   9. b   10. d
11. b   12. b   13. d   14. d   15. d   16. a   17. a   18. d   19. d   20. a
21. d   22. b   23. b   24. a   25. d   26. a   27. d   28. d

Chapter 8
1. c   2. d   3. a   4. c   5. c   6. d   7. a   8. c   9. c   10. b
11. b   12. d   13. d   14. d   15. b

Chapter 9
1. d   2. a   3. c   4. b   5. c   6. d   7. c   8. c   9. d   10. d
11. d   12. d   13. d   14. a   15. d   16. d   17. a   18. d   19. b   20. d
21. d   22. d   23. d   24. d   25. b   26. a   27. d   28. d   29. d

www.ingramcontent.com/pod-product-compliance
Lightning Source LLC
Chambersburg PA
CBHW081849230426
43669CB00018B/2877